D0616852

Bittersweet Within My Heart

THE COLLECTED POEMS *of* MARY, QUEEN OF SCOTS

Mary, Queen of Scots, wearing 'a carnation habit' and putting on the wedding ring she received from the Dauphin Francis in 1558. Portrait by an unknown artist.

Bittersweet Within My Heart

THE
COLLECTED
POEMS *of*
MARY, QUEEN
OF SCOTS

TRANSLATED & EDITED BY
ROBIN BELL

I could not have prepared this book without the practical assistance of Maria Blasquez, who gave invaluable help with translations and provided advice and encouragement throughout the project

The editor and publisher acknowledge support from The Scottish Arts Council towards the publication of this volume.

First published in Great Britain in 1992 by
PAVILION BOOKS LIMITED
196 Shaftesbury Avenue, London WC2H 8JL

Translation and selection © Robin Bell 1992

The moral right of the translator/editor has been asserted

Designed by Peter Luff

All rights reserved. No part of this publication may be reproduced, stored in a retrieval system, or transmitted, in any form or by any means, electronic, mechanical, photocopying, recording or otherwise, without the prior permission of the copyright holder

A CIP catalogue record for this book
is available from the British Library

ISBN 1 85145 9103

Printed and bound in Italy by New Interlitho

2 4 6 8 10 9 7 5 3 1

This book may be ordered by post direct from the publisher. Please contact the Marketing Department. But try your bookshop first.

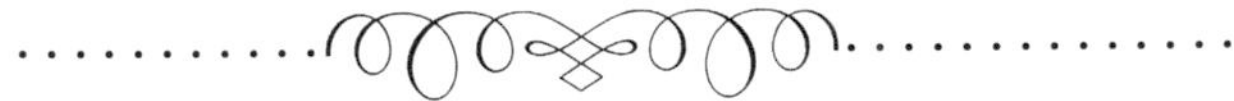

CONTENTS

VERSE CONTENTS

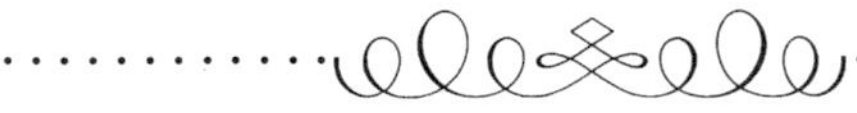

WHAT I WAS I NO MORE REMAIN

Verses Written in Her Book of Hours:

Did any more ill-fated.
Qui jamais davantage.

My fame, unlike in former days.
Comme autres fois la renommée.

I guide the hours and guide the day.
Les heures je guide et le jour.

Since she makes honour.
Celle que d'honneur sait combler.

Never again in all my fame must I.
Il faut plus que la renommée.

A heart which suffers agony.
Un coeur, que l'outrage martyre.

If our thoughts rise heavenward.
Si nos pensers sont élevés.

For the reward and salary.
Pour récompense et pour salaire.

With feigned good will.
En feinte mes amis changent .

None has the right.
Il n'appartient porter ces armes.

Time is more use to us.
Bien plus utile est l'heure.

Old age is an ill.
La vieillesse est un mal.

Verses:

A man is lacking in civility.
Celui vraiment n'a point de courtoisie.

The gods, the heavens, death.
Les dieux, les cieux, la mort.

TRIAL AND EXECUTION

Sonnet in Prison I:
O Lord my God, receive my prayer.
O Seigneur Dieu, recevez ma prière.

Sonnet in Prison II:
Give me, O Lord, the patience.
Donne, Seigneur, donne-moi patience.

Verses to Ronsard:
Ronsard, if your good, gentle-natured heart.
Ronsard, si ton bon coeur.

Written in the Spa at Buxton Wells:
Buxton of whose hot springs I often tell.
Buxtona, quae calidae celebrans nomen lymphae.

Composed During the Morning Before Her Execution:
O my Lord and my God, I have trusted in Thee.
O Domine Deus speravi in Te.

Sonnet Written at Fotheringhay Castle:
What am I? What use has my life?
Que suis-je hélas? Et de quoi sert ma vie?

FOREWORD

THE REAL MARY, QUEEN OF SCOTS, has been allowed to disappear under the weight of words written about her. The purpose of this book is to let her speak up for herself in her *own* words.

This is the first time that her complete poems have appeared in print. Some were well known in her lifetime. Others were secretly noted in the margins of her prayer book or crowded on to sheets of paper while she was in prison. The manuscripts and early printed versions are widely scattered. I will not weary the reader with details of how I established the authenticity of each poem.

I have modernized the spelling and punctuation to let readers have easy access to her writing without having to struggle with the inconsistent orthography of the original manuscripts. The dates that I give with the poems are the best approximations I can make, except in a few cases where the original text carried a precise date.

I chose to write verse translations rather than play safe and stick to plain prose. The reason is that the rhymes and rhythms of Mary's words give as much of a sense of

the woman as do their meanings. The style of her poems is often a key to her mental state and I felt I had to do my best to render her poems as fully as possible into a range of English with which she would have been familiar. I have tried to be faithful to both her strengths and her weaknesses, but no doubt I have fallen short in many cases.

To help the reader enjoy Mary, Queen of Scots', writing more fully and avoid an irritating clutter of footnotes, I have written a short commentary giving the private and political context for each poem. In order to show how our vision of Mary has evolved, the illustrations include both strong contemporary portraits and later romantic images.

What was she really like? Was she a serious, devout woman with a powerful sense of duty, or was she a frivolous schemer unable to control her passions? Her own words may help you decide.

Robin Bell

CHAPTER ONE

Daughter of the Auld Alliance

MARY WAS BORN IN LINLITHGOW PALACE on 8 December 1542. Six days later she became queen of Scotland when her father King James V died, worn out by the troubles of his kingdom and the crushing defeat inflicted by the English on his army at Solway Moss. James had wanted a son. He knew that a female heir would grow up tormented by intrigue at home and abroad to win her hand in marriage and control her kingdom.

Scotland's warring nobles exploited the conflict between Protestants and Catholics for their own ends. At first the Protestant faction held control and agreed that the infant Mary should marry Prince Edward, heir to the English throne. Mary's mother, the Catholic Mary of Guise, preferred 'the auld alliance' between her own

Opposite: *Mary, Queen of Scots, 'in white mourning' for the death of her husband, King Francis II. Panel by an unknown artist, 1560.*

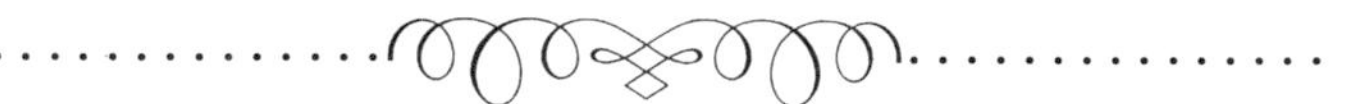

France and Scotland and sent Mary to France to be betrothed to the Dauphin Francis, heir to King Henry II. She was still only five years old.

At the French court, Mary received the training appropriate for a cultivated European princess. She learned Latin, Greek, Italian and Spanish as well as English. French, however, was her preferred language for the rest of her life.

Even at that most sophisticated of courts, Mary had a poise and charm that made her stand out. She was admired and popular for her unusual combination of modest piety and royal authority, scholarly learning and love of music and dancing. Much of her time was spent at the palace of Fontainebleau, where royal patronage attracted the best musicians of the day and encouraged the new school of allegorical artists who painted serious classical themes with a delicate eroticism.

Mary loved the gracious romance and ingenious wordplay of contemporary poetry. She was fortunate to have as her literary mentor Pierre de Ronsard, one of the greatest of all French poets, who remained her friend for life. When she began to write poetry herself, she followed his way of combining deceptively simple language and honest self-examination with deft puns and subtle wordgames. She had a fine ear for the rhythms of speech and a sound grasp of metre and rhyme. She rarely had

time or patience to polish her writing and sometimes her characteristic sideways leaps in thought fit badly within strict verse forms. At their best, her poems have a freshness and urgency that rank with the best writers of her day.

She married the Dauphin Francis in 1558 when she was fifteen and he was fourteen years old. On 10 July 1559, Henry II died after a jousting accident and Mary found herself queen of France as well as Scotland. After the death of the English Queen Mary the next year, she also had a claim by birthright to the throne of England and was a serious rival to Elizabeth I. She was still only seventeen. Everything was in her favour.

Suddenly disaster struck twice. Her mother, Mary of Guise, who had been an adroit politician in Scotland on Mary's behalf, died on 11 June 1560. On 5 December, Francis II died of an ear infection, the kind of illness that today would be quickly cured by antibiotics.

There was no useful role for a teenage royal widow at the French court. On 19 August 1561, Mary set sail to take up her birthright as queen of Scotland, well aware of its political turmoil and religious division, stirred up by the fiery John Knox, whose treatise 'On The Monstrous Regiment of Women' showed exactly what many Scots thought of the idea of a female monarch.

The daughter of the auld alliance was on her own.

Quatrain écrit dans le livre de Messe de sa tante Anne de Lorraine, La duchesse d'Aerschot.

Si ce lieu est pour écrire ordonné
Ce qu'il vous plaît avoir en souvenance,
Je vous requiers que lieu me soit donné
Et que nul temps m'en ôte l'ordonnance.

Reine de France Marie.

MARY WAS SEVENTEEN *when she wrote this poem. She was queen of the dazzling court of France and was at the height of her happiness and security.*

This poem contains the first known example of Mary's fondness for wordplay. She plays on ordonné/ordonnance, just as eight years later she plays on sujets/assujettie in the sonnet to Bothwell 'Entre ses mains et en son plein pouvoir'.

Quatrain Written in the Mass Book Belonging to Her Aunt Anne of Lorraine, Duchess of Aerschot. *1559*

If I am ordered to write in this space
Because you're pleased by such a souvenir,
I ask of you always to save my place
And ne'er withdraw the order I have here.

Mary Queen of France.

King James V and Mary of Guise, the parents of Mary, Queen of Scots. Portrait by an unknown artist.

Ode on the Death of Her Husband, King Francis II, When He Was Sixteen and She Was Seventeen Years Old. *1560*

In my sad, quiet song,
A melancholy air,
I shall look deep and long
At loss beyond compare,
And with bitter tears,
I'll pass my best years.

Have the harsh fates ere
now
Let such a grief be felt,
Has a more cruel blow
Been by Dame Fortune
dealt
Than, O my heart and
eyes!
I see where his bier lies?

In my springtime's
gladness
And flower of my young
heart,
I feel the deepest sadness
Of the most grievous hurt.
Nothing now my heart can
fire
But regret and desire.

He who was my dearest
Already is my plight.
The day that shone the
clearest
For me is darkest night.
There's nothing now so
fine
That I need make it mine.

Deep in my eyes and heart
A portrait has its place
Which shows the world my
hurt
In the pallor of my face,
Pale as when violets fade,
True love's becoming
shade.

In my unwonted pain

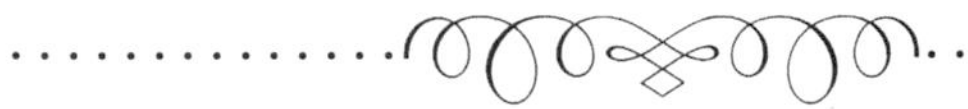

I can no more be still,
Rising time and again
To drive away my ill.
All things good and bad
Have lost the taste they
had.

And thus I always stay
Whether in wood or
meadow,
Whether at dawn of day
Or at the evening shadow.
My heart feels ceaselessly
Grief for his loss to me.

Sometimes in such a place
His image comes to me
The sweet smile on his
face
Up in a cloud I see.

FRANCIS AND MARY grew up together at the French court. In an era of dynastic weddings between strangers, they were happy that childhood friendship was allowed to grow into a royal marriage.

When he died of an ear infection, Mary was distraught. Her whole training from the age of five had been for a career as queen of France. Now, a week before her eighteenth birthday, that role was over and she had lost the husband she loved.

She turned to poetry to express her grief. She is not afraid to show her vulnerability, but her sense of duty and dignity give her the strength to confront her emotions with extraordinary maturity. The two great court poets Ronsard and Brantôme regarded this poem highly.

In the fifth verse, Mary says she became pale through grief. Brantôme said, 'Never after she was a widow, during all the time that I had the honour to see her in France and in Scotland, was her complexion restored.'

Then sudden in the mere
I see his funeral bier.

When I lie quietly
Sleeping upon my couch,
I hear him speak to me
And I can feel his touch.
In my duties each day
He is near me alway.

Nothing seems fine to me
Unless he is therein.
My heart will not agree
Unless he is within.
I lack all perfection
In my cruel dejection.

I shall cease my song now,
My sad lament shall end
Whose burden aye shall
show
True love can not pretend
And, though we are apart,
Grows no less in my heart.

Ode sur la mort de son mari, Le Roi François II, quand il avait seize ans et elle avait dix-sept ans.

En mon triste et doux
chant
D'un ton fort lamentable,
Je jette un oeil tranchant,
De perte incomparable,
Et en soupirs cuisants
Passe mes meilleurs ans.

Fut-il un tel malheur
De dure destinée
Ni si triste douleur
De Dame Fortunée
Qui, mon coeur et mon
oeil,
Vois en bière et cercueil?

Qui en mon doux
printemps

Et fleur de ma jeunesse
Toutes les peines sens
D'une extrême tristesse,
Et en rien n'ai plaisir
Qu'en regret et désir.

Ce qui m'était plaisant
Ores m'est peine dure;*
*maintenant
Le jour le plus luisant
M'est nuit noire et
obscure;
Et n'est rien si exquis
Qui de moi soit requis.

J'ai au coeur et à l'oeil
Un portrait et image
Qui figure mon deuil
Et mon pâle visage
*De violettes teint** *éteintes
Qui est l'amoureux teint

Pour mon mal étranger
Je ne m'arrête en place,
Mais j'en ai beau changer
Si ma douleur efface;* *ainsi
Car mon pis et mon mieux
Sont mes plus déserts
lieux.

Si en quelque séjour,
Soit en bois ou en pré,
Soit pour l'aube du jour
Ou soit pour la vesprée,*
*le soir
Sans cesse mon coeur sent
Le regret d'un absent.

Si parfois vers ces lieux
Viens à dresser ma vue,
Le doux trait de ses yeux
Je vois en une nue,
Soudain je vois en l'eau
Comme dans un tombeau.

Si je suis en repos,
Sommeillante sur ma
couche
J'ois qu'il me tient*
propos; *j'entends
Je le sens qu'il me touche;
En labeur, en reçoi,*
*recevoir à la cour
Toujours est près de moi.

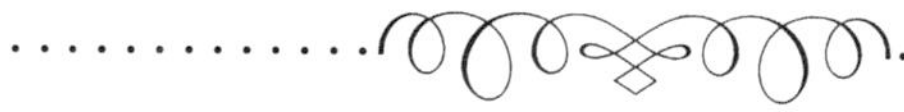

Je ne vois autre objet
Pour beau qu'il se
présente;
A quel que soit sujet
Oncques mon coeur*
consente, **jamais*
Exempte de perfection
A cette affliction.

Mets chanson ici fin
A si triste complainte
Dont sera le refrain:
Amour vrai et non feint
Pour la séparation
N'aura diminution.

The Dauphin Francis, aged fourteen, at the time he married Mary, Queen of Scots. Chalk drawing by François Clouet.

The Diamond Speaks. *1562*

'Tis not because my strength outranks both flame and
brand,
Nor because my facets display a cunning hand,
Nor because, set in fine-wrought gold, I shine so bright,
Nor even that I'm pure, whiter than Phoebus' light,
But rather because my form is a heart, like unto
My Mistress' heart (but for hardness), that I'm sent to you.
For all things must yield to unfettered purity
And she is my true equal in each quality.
For who would fail to grant that once I had been sent,
My Mistress should thus, in turn, find favour and
content?
May it please, from these omens I shall gather strength
And thus from Queen to equal Queen I'll pass at length.
O would I could join them with an iron band alone
(Though all prefer gold) and unite their hearts as one
That neither envy, greed nor gossip's evil play,
Nor mistrust, nor ravaging time could wear away.
Then they'd say among treasures I was most renowned,
For I'd have two great jewels in one setting bound.
Then with my glitt'ring rays I should confound the sight
Of all who saw me, dazzling enemies with my light.
Then, by my worth and by her art, I should be known
As the diamond, the greatest jewel, the mighty stone.

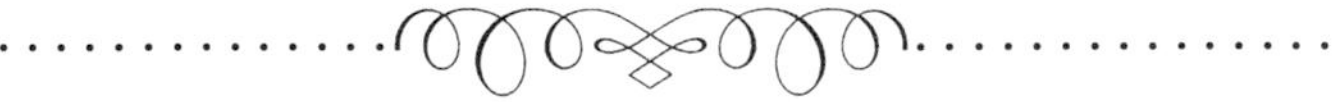

Adamas Loquitur. 1562

Non quia duritia superem ferrumque focumque,
Sculpta, nec artificis glorior ipsa manu,
Nec quia gemma nitens operoso cingar ab auro
Pura quidem, et Phoebi sidere candidior:
Sed potius cordi similis mea forma, quod ipsum
Cor Dominae, excepta duritie, exhibeat.
Nam quod ab oppositis non vincitur et sine noedis
Candida quod tota est? His ego, et illa, pareis.
Cedere quis possit? postquam me emiserat illa
Mi Dominam rursus posse placere nonam?

Queen Elizabeth I of England in 1559. Portrait by an unknown artist.

Sed placet: hoc faustae foelix en debeo forti,
Me Regina iterum, nec minor ista, tenet.
O utinam ambarum bene possum adamantina vincla,
(Ore fauete omnes) cordibus injucere.
Quae neque liuor edax, neque falsis acta susurris
Suspicio, aut caries temporis ulla, terant.
Tunc ego ab Eois dicar celeberrima gazis,
Hic etiam gemmas vincere praecipuas.
Tunc ego perstringam tremulo fulgore coruscans,
Adstantum, immisis lumina seu radus.
Tunc ego seu pretio, seu quae me provocet arte,
Gemma, adamas firmo robore prima ferar.

Translated by Sir Thomas Chaloner

ELIZABETH I SAW MARY *as a dangerous rival whose claim to the throne of England could be exploited by the Catholic faction in Britain and Mary's allies in France and Spain. She told the unmarried Elizabeth she wished to be considered as her heir, but had no wish to usurp her throne, and sent her this poem with a diamond ring as a token of friendship.*

Mary's original French poem is lost. All that remain are two different Latin translations, one published by Sir Thomas Chaloner in 1579 and the other published by George Conn in 1624. My English reconstruction is therefore two stages removed from Mary's own words. I have guessed that she wrote this poem in rhyming couplets, such as she used for her 'Meditation', but I could be wrong.

Adamas Loquitur

Non me materies facit superbum
Quod ferro insuperabilis, quod ignis
Non candor macula carens, nitoris
Non lux perspicui, nec ars magistri
Qui formam dedit hanc, loquaci
Circumvestuit eleganter auro:
Sed quod cor Dominae meae figurae
Tam certa exprimo pectore ut recluso
Cor si luminibus quaeat videri,
Cor non lumina certius viderent.
Sic constantia firma cordi utrique
Sic candor macula carens, nitoris
Sic lux perspicui, nihil doli intus

It is worth comparing this poem to the one Mary wrote to Elizabeth six years later. In both, Mary is conciliatory and anxious, an error of judgement when addressing Elizabeth, who respected strength and trampled on weakness.

Lord Randolph in a letter to Lord Cecil, dated 17 June 1562, quotes Mary as saying: 'Above everything, I desire to see my good sister (Elizabeth I) and next that we may live like good sisters together . . . I have a ring with a diamond fashioned like a heart; I know nothing that can resemble my good will unto my sister better than that. My meaning shall be expressed by writing, in a few verses which you shall see before you depart.' These are the verses.

Celans, omnia denique aequa praeter
Unam duritiem dein secundus
Hic gradus mihi fortis est faventus,
Talem Heroida quod videre sperem
Qualem mihi spes nulla erat videndi
Antiqua Domina semel relicta,
Osi fors mihi faxit utriusque
Nectam ut corda adamantina catena
Quam nec suspicio, aemulatiove
Livorve, aut odium aut senecta solvat.
Tam beatior omnibus lapillis
Tam sum clarior omnibus lapillis
Tam sum durior omnibus lapillis.

Translated by George Conn

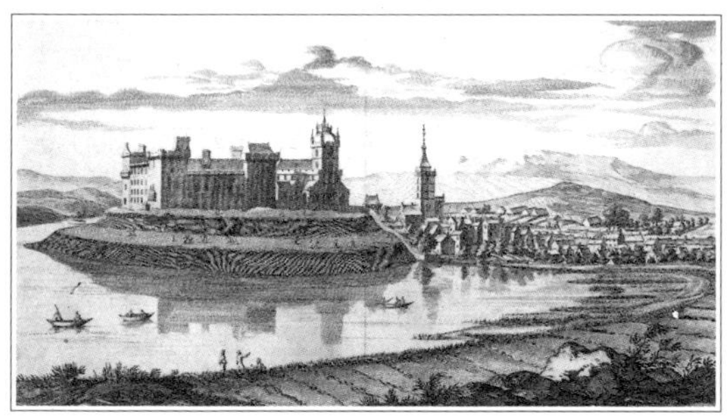

Linlithgow Palace. Birthplace of Mary, Queen of Scots.
Engraving by Captain John Slezer.

CHAPTER TWO

Poems of Love and Jealousy

MARY NEEDED A HUSBAND to provide an heir to the throne and put an end to the dynastic manoeuvres that destabilized Scotland. The poet-queen fell in love with her Stewart cousin Henry, Lord Darnley, who wooed her with poems of his own. They married on 29 July 1565. He was eighteen. She was twenty-two.

On 19 June 1566, Mary gave birth to a son, James. Scotland had an heir and, since Elizabeth I was unmarried, James was heir to the English throne as well. Meanwhile, Darnley's dissolute behaviour and indifference to affairs of state made him a political liability.

On 10 February 1567, an explosion destroyed the house in which Darnley was staying in Edinburgh. He was found strangled in the garden. Who killed him? The main suspect was the Earl of Bothwell, Mary's chief

Opposite: *Mary and her Italian secretary, David Riccio, who shared her love of poetry. A Victorian 'history' painting by J R Herbert.*

adviser and close friend. He was charged with murder but acquitted when he appeared for trial in Edinburgh accompanied by a small army who made it plain to John Manderstoun, canon of Dunbar, that 'there shall not fail to be noses and lugges (ears) cut and far greater displeasures' if Bothwell did not get what he wanted.

Bothwell was powerful and ruthless. Mary, widowed for the second time, began to see him as the strong consort she needed to govern Scotland and protect her infant son. He saw her as a means of becoming king.

On 24 April 1567, Bothwell persuaded Mary to come to Dunbar Castle where he raped her. Contemporary accounts say that Mary was already at a low ebb, physically and mentally. She found herself helplessly attracted to Bothwell and agreed to marry him as soon as he divorced his current wife, Lady Jean. Once she had made her decision, Mary needed to persuade herself her commitment was justified despite her moral beliefs. She turned again to poetry to release her feelings. When she began writing sonnets to Bothwell, the floodgates of love and jealousy opened. Emotions, ranging from a noble desire for honour to sneering petty spite, rushed out.

The sonnets became the centre of a political storm. On 17 June 1567, Bothwell's servant George Dalgleish was seized by Mary's enemy, the Earl of Morton. Under threat of torture he produced a silver casket, filled with

Bothwell's personal papers. We shall never know just what was in the casket because the original documents were soon destroyed. It was claimed to contain not only these sonnets but letters incriminating Mary in Darnley's murder. Historians are generally agreed now that these 'casket letters' were faked by her enemies. The Bothwell sonnets, however, are consistent with Mary's characteristic, slightly unorthodox syntax and her wordgames, puns, sideways leaps in thought and conventional piety mixed with deep emotion. They have the same themes of duty, devotion, honour, constancy and suffering that recur in her later writing. They are also the first sonnets she wrote. Enemies faking poems would have been far more likely to copy her earlier ode or rhyming couplets, rather than guess the form she would adopt later in her career!

That said, the sonnets may have been tampered with and their order shuffled. George Buchanan, a fine Latin scholar and a treacherous opportunist, who wrote sycophantic poems of praise to her then switched sides politically just before her downfall, claimed they were written *before* Darnley's murder. He prepared 'Ane Detection of the Duinges of Marie, Quene of Scottis, Touchand the Murder of hir Husband' in which he used the sonnets to add credibility to a mass of hearsay and speculative 'evidence'. Mary's private poems were now public.

O dieux ayez de moi compassion
Et m'enseignez quelle preuve certaine* *quelque
Je puis donner qui ne lui semble vaine
de mon amour et ferme affection.
Las n'est-il pas déjà en possession* *hélas
Du corps, du coeur qui ne refuse peine
Ni déshonneur en la vie incertaine,
Offense des parents, ni pire affliction?
Pour lui tous mes amis j'estime moins que rien
Et de mes ennemis je veux espérer bien.
J'ai hasardé pour lui et nom et conscience:
Je veux pour lui au monde renoncer:
Je veux mourir pour lui avancer.
Que reste il plus pour prouver ma constance?

Mary's third husband, James Hepburn, Earl of Bothwell, and Bothwell's first wife, Lady Jean Gordon. Painted by an unknown artist in 1566.

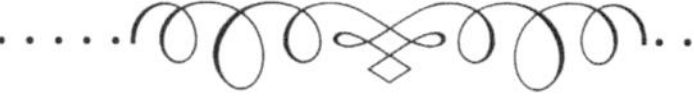

Twelve Sonnets to Lord Bothwell.

APRIL TO JUNE 1567

1.

Lord, grant your mercy unto me:
Teach me some way that he may know
My love for him is not an empty show
But purest tenderness and constancy.
For does he not, alas, ev'n now possess
This body and this heart which would not flee
Discord, dishonour, nor uncertainty,
Nor family hurt, nor evil's worst distress.
For his sake, I value all my friends as dust
And in my enemies I seek to place my trust.
For him, my conscience and good name to chance I've cast:
I would renounce the world, were it his whim:
I'd gladly die if it should profit him.
What more is there to prove my love steadfast?

MARY WAS COMMITTED TO BOTHWELL, *but he believed she was merely making the best of things after the rape and that her feelings as a woman were no more than a show put on to manipulate him. Mary wanted more than his political power. She needed his trust to salve her religious conscience and her self-respect. In this poem, she tries to come to terms with how she has alienated her Scottish Stewart relatives and their allies, confronting her feelings with a terrified honesty.*

Elle, pour son honneur, vous doit obéissance.
Moi, vous obéissant, j'en puis recevoir blâme,
N'étant, à mon regret, comme elle, votre femme.
Et si n'aura pourtant en ce point préeminence* *même si
Pour son profit elle use de constance,
Car ce n'est peu d'honneur, d'être de vos biens dame.
Et moi, pour vous aimer, j'en puis recevoir blâme.
Et ne lui veut céder en toute l'observance.
Elle, de votre mal, n'a l'apprehénsion;
Moi, j'ai nul repos tant je crains l'apparence.
Par l'avis des parents, elle eut votre accointance.
Moi, malgré tous les miens, vous porte affection.
Et toutefois, mon coeur, vous doutez ma constance
Et de sa loyauté prenez ferme assurance.

'SHE' IS BOTHWELL'S WIFE, *Lady Jean Gordon, whom he had married on 24 February 1566, little more than a year before this poem was written. The marriage allied him to the powerful Huntly family and Jean's dowry helped towards the debts he had incurred, according to Buchanan, 'at dice and among harlottes'.*

Now Bothwell's ambitions were higher: he wanted to marry the queen herself and had gained Mary's consent if only he could get rid of his current wife. When Mary wrote this poem, Bothwell was seeking

2.

She does your bidding for her honour's sake.
I do your bidding and have naught but strife
Since, unlike her, alas, I'm not your wife.
And though this precedence she cannot take,
She uses constancy to benefit her name
– For there's small honour as mere mistress of your
 house –
While I, for loving you, receive only abuse.
And I will not give way to her, nor play her game.
She does not grasp the danger you are in;
I cannot rest for fear of what may be.
She made your aquaintance through her family;
I bring you love and thus defy my kin.
But nonetheless you doubt if I be true
And place your trust in her loyalty to you.

an annulment from Jean on grounds of consanguinity. As a devout Catholic, Mary did not approve of divorce.

Jean, however, cross-petitioned for divorce from Bothwell on the grounds of his adultery with Bessie Crawford, her mother's sewing maid. By acting the wronged wife, Jean hoped to negotiate a better financial settlement. Meanwhile, Mary found herself in the undignified role of an amorous interloper, her feelings disregarded by her social inferiors.

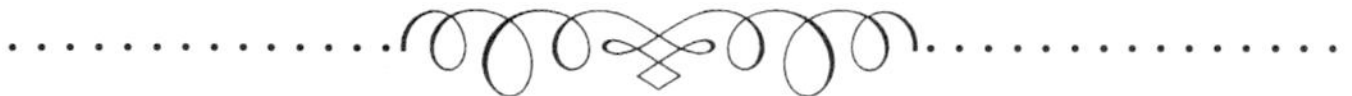

Par vous, mon coeur, et par votre alliance
Elle a remis sa maison en honneur.
Elle a joui par vous de la grandeur
Dont tous les siens n'ont nulle assurance.
De vous, mon bien, elle a eu la constance
Et a gagné pour un temps votre coeur.
Par vous elle a eu plaisir et bonheur,
Et par vous a reçu honneur et révérence;
Et n'a perdu sinon la jouissance
D'un fâcheux sot qu'elle aimait chèrement.
Je ne la plains d'aimer donc ardemment* *blâme pas
Celui qui n'a en sens, ni en vaillance,
En beauté, en bonté, ni en constance,
Point de seconde. Je vis en cette foi.

THE 'TIRESOME DOLT' *in line ten is Alexander Ogilvy of Boyne. He and Jean Gordon had planned to marry, but her Huntly relatives preferred a dynastic alliance with Bothwell, linking the North with the Borders. Jean submitted but annoyed her new husband by wearing mourning dress to lament her old love. Alexander, less sentimentally, promptly married Mary Beaton, one of the 'four Marys' who were ladies-in-waiting to the queen.*

3.

Through you, my heart, and through your marriage vow,
She has restored her honour and estate;
She has achieved through you a rank more great
Than any of her kin could hope to know.
From you, my joy, she has had steadfast love
And for a time she's occupied your heart.
Through you, pleasure in good fortune is her part
And, through you, others honour and approve.
She's had to give up nothing, save the embrace
Of a tiresome dolt she once loved dear;
I don't condemn her love that burns so clear
For one who, in wisdom, gallantry and grace,
In generous heart and in constancy
Is second to none. I live in that faith.

. . . .

Thirty years later, Jean got her man. After divorcing Bothwell, Jean married the Earl of Sutherland and, upon his death, finally married Alexander Ogilvy.

Sometimes Mary could not think of a good ending to a poem. In this sonnet, she made a note 'I live in that faith', intending to replace it later with a phrase that rhymed and scanned. Events moved so fast in the early summer of 1560 that she never had the time or peace of mind to revise what she had written.

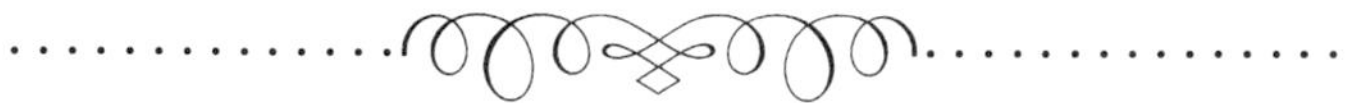

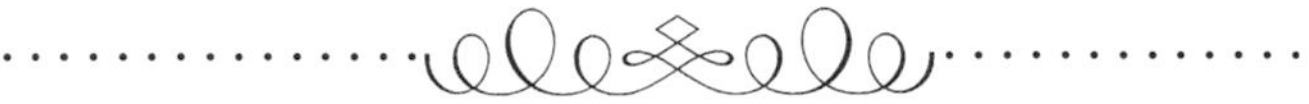

Mon amour croît et plus en plus croîtra
Tant que je vivrai et tiendra à grandeur
Tant seulement d'avoir part en ce coeur
Vers qui enfin mon amour paraîtra
Si très à clair que jamais n'en doutera.* *tellement
Pour lui je veux faire tête au malheur.* *tenir
Pour lui je veux rechercher la grandeur
Et ferai tant qu'en vrai connaîtra
Que je n'ai bien, heur, ni contentement,.* *bonheur
Qu'a l'obéir et servir loyalement.
Pour lui j'attends toute bonne fortune.
Pour lui je veux garder santé et vie.
Pour lui tout vertu de suivre j'ai envie.
Et sans changer me trouvera toute une.

MARY, THROUGHOUT HER LIFE, *was obsessed with having her emotions recognized as genuine. It is a recurrent theme in her letters. Seven years earlier, in her ode on the death of Francis II, she refers to 'amour vraye et non fainte'. Six years after the above sonnet she wrote another, 'L'ire de Dieu', which is a religious parallel to her theme of how devoted love should be expressed.*

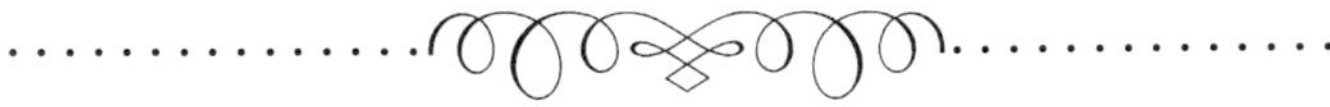

4.

My love for him is growing and shall grow
Throughout my life as long as there's a part
Where it can grow to greatness in that heart;
Then at the last my love may show
So very clearly he shall have no doubt.
For him I'll undergo the worst ordeal.
For him, I'll seek out honour with all zeal,
And through my deeds for certain he'll find out
That wealth, content and ease are lost to me
Unless I do his will and serve him loyally.
For him, I seek good chance from fortune's store.
For him, I wish to keep my life and thrive;
For him, to follow virtue's path I'll strive;
And he will find me constant evermore.

The perspective in the Bothwell sonnets varies; sometimes she speaks direct to Bothwell, sometimes she asks God to help her. In this sonnet, she engages in a dialogue with herself, as if she were looking in a mirror, trying to reassure the doubts of the woman facing her.

Pour lui aussi j'ai jeté mainte larme.
Premier, quand il se fit de ce corps possesseur,
Duquel alors il n'avait pas le coeur.
Puis me donna une autre dure alarme
*Quand il versa de son sang mainte dragme** **unité de mesure*
Dont de grief il me vint laisser** douleur* **chagrin **fuir*
Qu'il me pensa ôter la vie et frayeur* **que je pensai*
De perdre las le seul rempart qui m'arme.* **hélas*
Pour lui depuis j'ai méprisé l'honneur
Ce qui nous peut seul pourvoir de bonheur.
Pour lui j'ai hasardé grandeur et conscience.
Pour lui tous mes parents j'ai quitté et amis,
Et tous autres respects sont à part mis.* **égards*
Brief, de vous seul je cherche l'alliance.

MARY BEGINS *by talking about Bothwell's raping her at Dunbar in April 1567. She also mentions an incident in the Borders in October 1566 when Bothwell was seriously wounded by Jock Elliot of the Park, the leader of a gang of cattle thieves. Mary rode thirty miles in foul weather to visit him at Hermitage. Buchanan says this shows she was already desperately in love with him, but in fact it was an official visit. Mary took with her Lords Moray, Huntly and Maitland, all of whom wanted to know if Bothwell, the hereditary governor of an*

5.

And I have shed for him so many a tear.
First when he took my body and made it his own
Although my heart was not yet won.
Again he filled me with great fear,
When so much of his blood spilled out
That, out of grief I thought to ease the pain
By ending my own life and ne'er fear again
The loss, alas, of my one true redoubt.
For him I've spurned my honour, and disdained
The only way true happiness is gained.
For him, I've gambled conscience, rank and right.
For him, all friends and family I've fled,
And all respectability I've shed:
In short, with you alone will I unite.

important part of the kingdom, was likely to survive his wounds.

The sonnet makes it clear that she cared for Bothwell but, if she was so distressed by the rape in April, it is hardly likely they had been lovers since the previous October. Also, her recollection of her feelings for Bothwell eight months before should not be relied upon too much. At the time she wrote this poem, it was hard enough for her to come to terms with her immediate emotions.

De vous je dis seul soutien de ma vie* *je vous appelle
Tant seulement je cherche m'assurer,
Et si ose de moi tant présumer* *ainsi
De vous gagner malgré tout l'ennui.
Car c'est le seul désir de votre chère amie
De vous servir et loyalement aimer
Et tout malheur moins que rien estimer
Et votre volonté de la mienne suivre.
Vous connaîtrez avec obéissance* *grâce à mon
De mon loyal devoir, n'omettant la science
A quoi j'étudierai pour toujours vous complaire,* *que
Sans aimer rien que vous, sous la sujétion
De qui je veux sans nulle fiction
Vivre et mourir et à ce j'obtempère.

ON 3 MAY 1567, Lady Jean Bothwell was granted a divorce by the Protestant Commissary Court. On 7 May, the Catholic Archbishop Hamilton also annulled the marriage. It was now possible for Mary and Bothwell to marry. The date was set for the following Thursday, 15 May.

As her wedding day drew closer, Mary increasingly tried to convince herself she was doing the right thing. Contemporaries describe her looking ill, alternately lacklustre and agitated. Sonnets five and

6.

I call you my sole sustenance of life
Only because I seek to make it true;
Thus I dare force myself in all I do
In order to win you despite all the strife.
For your dear friend has one desire alone:
To serve you and to love you loyally
And think nothing of adversity
And to your will subject my own.
You'll see how large a part obedience plays
In my devotion, and I will study always
The science of pleasing you most loyally;
Loving only you, a servant to your will,
I wish, with no pretence, to fulfil
My life and death, and with this I will comply.

six have an air of desperation.

The poem ends with 'j'obtempère', a word more often used by lawyers. It is possible that Mary's enemies tampered with the climax of the sonnet before showing these poems to English commissioners in 1568, with the suggestion that they were written before *Darnley's murder. In the Scottish legal establishment, devious dullards outnumber noble Ciceros.*

Entre ses mains et en son plein pouvoir
Je mets mon fils, mon honneur et ma vie,
Mon pays, mes sujets, mon âme assujettie
Et toute à lui, et n'ai autre vouloir
Pour mon objet que, sans le décevoir,
Suivre je veux, malgré tout l'ennui
Qu'issir en peut; car je n'ai autre envie* *résulter
Que, de ma foi, lui faire appercevoir
Que, pour tempête ou bonace qu'il fasse,
Jamais ne veux changer demeure ou place.
Bref, je ferai de ma foi telle preuve
Qu'il connaîtra sans feinte ma constance,
Non par mes pleurs ou feinte obéissance,
Comme autres ont fait, mais par diverses épreuves.

. . . .

ON 15 MAY, in the great hall at Holyrood, Mary and Bothwell were married by a Protestant minister. As a loyal Catholic, Mary had no faith in the ceremony – as she admitted later to her confessor, the

Previous page: *Mary, Queen of Scots, and Darnley at Jedburgh. A Victorian dramatic interpretation of the breakdown of Mary's second marriage. It is set in the time Mary mentions in sonnet five, when she rode thirty miles through wind and rain to visit the wounded Bothwell. Painted by Alfred Elmore in 1877.*

7.

Into his hands and wholly in his power
I place my son, my honour and my all,
My country, my subjects, my surrendered soul
And trust him with my life, and want no more
For my purpose than to follow his command,
And never fail him despite the suffering
That may attend, for I desire nothing
But, by my faith, to have him understand
Whatever weather, fair or foul, we face,
My love will never change its dwelling place.
In short, I'll prove my faith so he takes heed
And learns of my constancy, not by some pretence,
Nor artful sighs nor feigned obedience
As others have shown him, but by my every deed.

Bishop of Ross. In the line beginning 'Suivre je veux', Mary totally submits her royal will and lifelong training to the demands of her new husband.

Mary was on the edge of mental collapse. Sir James Melville says that on the following day he heard Mary ask for a knife to kill herself, and when her equerry Arthur Erskine tried to calm her, she said she would drown herself instead.

In the poem, the reference to her son, the future King James VI and I, is figurative. The infant prince was kept safe in Stirling Castle, rather than in Bothwell's personal care.

Quand vous l'aimiez, elle usait de froideur.
Si vous souffriez pour l'amour passion,* *à cause de
Qui vient d'aimer de trop d'affection,
Son doigt montrait la tristesse de coeur,
N'ayant plaisir de votre grande ardeur.
En ses habits, montrait sans fiction
Qu'elle n'avait peur qu'imperfection
Peut l'effacer hors de ce loyal coeur.
De votre mort je ne vis la peur
Que méritait tel mary et seigneur.* *mari
Somme, de vous elle a eu tout son bien* *En somme
Et n'a prisé ni jamais estimé
Un si grand heur puisqu'il n'est sien,* *bonheur
Et maintenant dit l'avoir tant aimé.

AFTER LADY JEAN GORDON divorced Bothwell, Mary remained jealous of her, with good reason. Though they were divorced, Bothwell kept his ex-wife handily accessible in Crichton Castle.

With Darnley and Bothwell, Mary could not cope emotionally when they showed affection to another woman. In this sonnet, her reaction is to belittle Jean, sneering at her frigidity and hypocrisy, implying that Mary was more willing and able to give sexual pleasure.

8.

While you made love, she lay with cold disdain.
If you were suffering the heat of passion
That comes from loving with too much emotion,
Her hand would make her heart's revulsion plain,
Taking no joy in your love's fervent art.
In her dress, she showed without a doubt,
She never feared bad taste might blot her out
From the affection of your loyal heart.
I saw in her none of the fear of death for you
That such a lord and husband should be due.
In short, though you're her source of all that's fair,
She never prized but valued very small
That finest hour because she failed to share,
Yet now she says she loved it best of all.

Mary's sarcastic remarks about Lady Jean Gordon's poor dress sense are particularly barbed, since Mary herself had sent eleven ells of silver cloth to make Lady Jean's wedding dress only the year before. To add to the irony, the same dress was sewn by Bessie Crawford, who became Bothwell's mistress and was cited in his divorce.

Et maintenant elle commence à voir
Qu'elle était bien de mauvais jugement
De n'estimer l'amour d'un tel amant;
Et voudrait bien mon ami décevoir
Par les écrits tout fardés de savoir,
*Qui pourtant n'est en son esprit croissant** *n'ont pas germé
Ains empruntés de quelque auteur éluissant.*** *Ainsi
**brillant
A fait très bien un envoi sans l'avoir.* *une missive
Et toutefois ses paroles fardées,
Ses pleurs, ses plaintes remplies de fictions,
Et ses hauts cris et lamentations,
Ont tant gagné que par vous sont gardées
Ses lettres écrites auxquelles vous donnez foi.
Et si l'aimez et croyez plus que moi.* *ainsi

ON 6 JUNE 1567, Bothwell and Mary retreated to Borthwick Castle. Lord Maitland inflamed Mary's jealousy by telling her that Bothwell had written to Jean, assuring her he still thought of her as his lawful wife. The French ambassador du Croc reported that everyone in Scotland believed Bothwell loved Jean 'more than he loves the queen'.

Mary hated the thought that a rival could match her in anything, and the sight of persuasively written letters from Jean to Bothwell infuriated her, all the more so because 'quelque autheur éluissant' shows that Mary could not identify from which author, if any, Jean had cribbed her words.

9.

And now at last she starts to comprehend
How poor her judgement was and to discover
She should not undervalue such a lover;
And she would fain deceive my friend
With writings tricked out in a learned tone
That could not be the product of her brain
But borrowed from the works of some great man.
She's sent a fine dispatch though she has none.
Nonetheless, her words painted to deceive,
Her tears, her fiction-laden piteous sighs,
Her lamentations, bawling cries,
Have worked their way so well that you believe
She wrote these letters and you save them carefully;
And thus you love and trust her more than me.

John Knox, the leading Scottish Protestant reformer. Woodcut by an unknown artist.

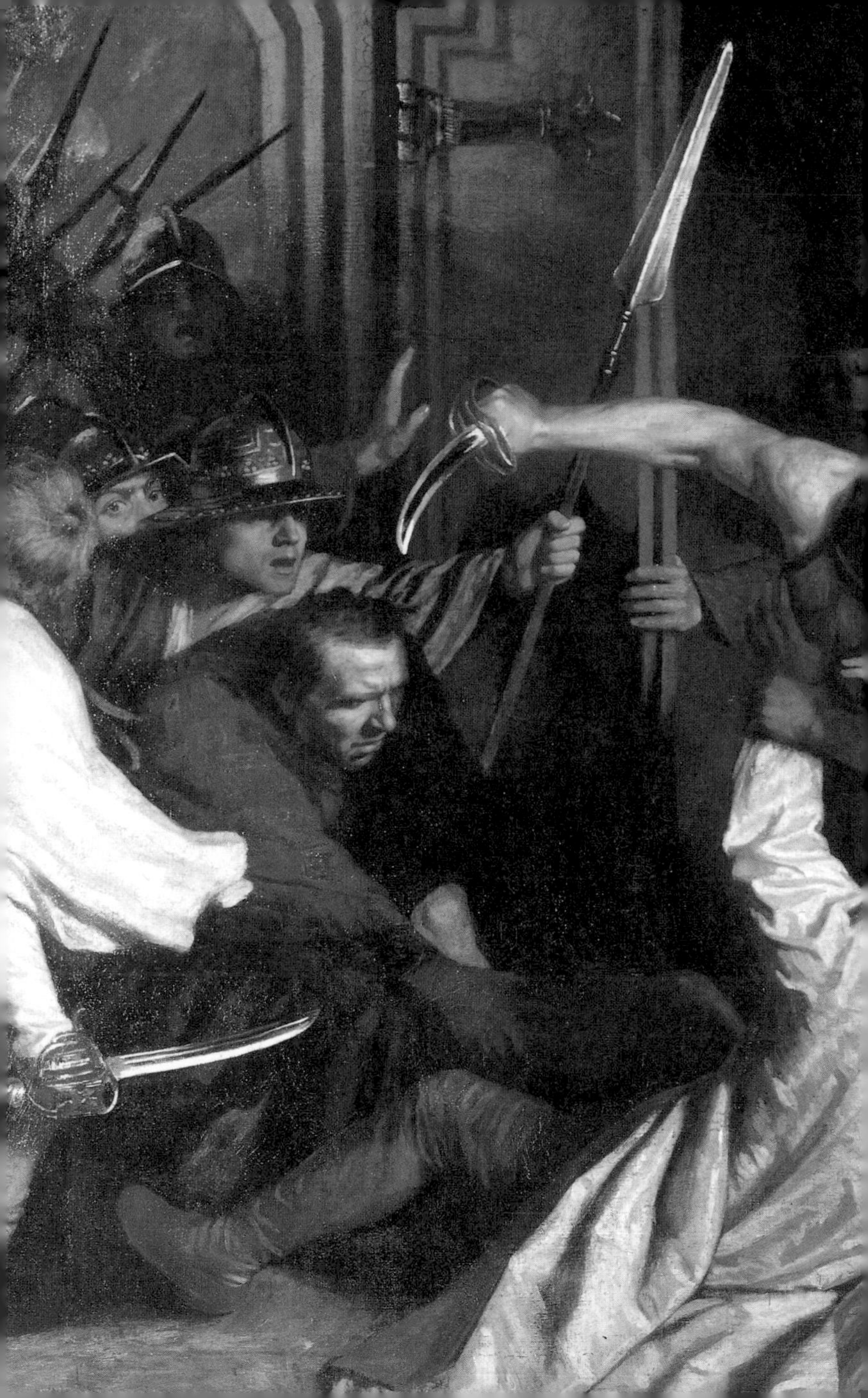

Vous la croyez, las! Trop je l'aperçois* *hélas
Et vous doutez de ma ferme constance,
O mon seul bien et ma seul espérance.
Et ne vous puis assurer de ma foi.
Vous m'estimez légère: qui le voit?* *ne (manque)
Et si n'avez en moi nulle assurance* *ainsi
Et soupçonnez mon coeur sans apparence,
Vous défiant à trop grand tort de moi.
Vous ignorez l'amour que je vous porte.
Vous soupçonnez qu'autre amour me transporte.
Vous estimez mes paroles du vent.
Vous dépeignez de cire mon las coeur.
Vous me pensez femme sans jugement.
Et tout cela augmente mon ardeur.

WHEN BOTHWELL LEFT MARY *at Borthwick while he tried to rally forces at Dunbar, he placed an armed guard at her chamber door. This may have been for Mary's safety, but she thought it was out of jealousy*

Previous page: *The Death of Riccio. David Riccio was a clever and ambitious Italian who became secretary to Mary, Queen of Scots, in Edinburgh. The Scottish nobles, including Mary's husband Darnley, became jealous of Riccio's increasing influence and favour with the queen. Darnley conspired to have him murdered in Holyrood Palace on 9 March 1566 in front of Mary, who was six months pregnant with the future Prince James. A Romantic drama painting by John Opie in 1787.*

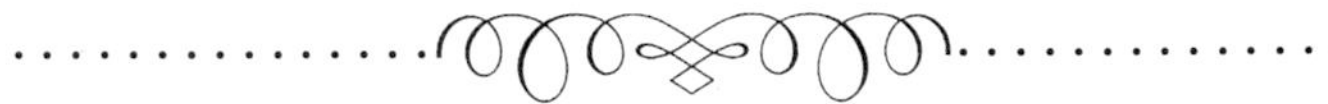

10.

You trust in her; alas I see too well you do!
And you cast doubt upon my constancy,
(You, who are the only joy and hope for me.)
And I cannot persuade you I am true.
You think I'm fickle, it's plain to see,
And thus you will not grant your confidence.
You mistrust my heart without evidence,
And your suspicion does great wrong to me.
You do not heed the love I bear at all.
You suspect some other love has me in thrall.
You value all my words no more than wind.
You picture my sad heart malleable as clay.
You think I am a woman with no mind.
All that makes love burn fiercer day by day.

and in turn wondered what Bothwell was up to with Jean while he was absent from Borthwick.

Mary was very sensitive about being thought fickle or frivolous and in line five defends herself, just as she does in line ten of her poem on the Bishop of Ross's Consolationes.

'Vous ignorez l'amour que je vous porte' in line nine is perhaps the most poignant of all Mary's punning wordgames. By early June, she realized she was pregnant by Bothwell. It tortured her to think that he still could not see, or would not care, how much she had placed her faith and her future in his hands.

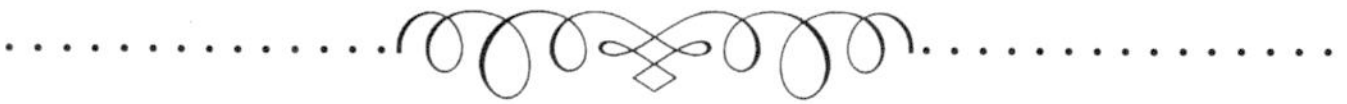

Mon coeur, mon sang, mon âme et mon souci,
Las, vous m'avez promis qu'aurions ce plaisir* *Hélas
De deviser avec vous à loisir
Toute la nuit où je languis ici,
Ayant le coeur d'extrême peur transi
Pour voir absent le but de mon désir.
Crainte d'oubli un coup** me vient à saisir* *d'être oubliée
**brusquement
Et l'autrefois je crains que rendurci
Soit contre moi votre aimable coeur
Par quelque dit d'un méchant rapporteur.* *médisance
Une autre fois je crains quelque aventure
Qui par chemin détourne mon amant
Par un fâcheux et nouveau accident.
Dieu détourne tout malheureux augure!

11.

My heart, my blood, my soul and my great care,
Alas you promised we should have the pleasure
Of whiling away the hours at leisure
All night long with you; but I languish here,
My heart pierced through by fear's most wounding dart,
Because I know not where my heart's desire may be.
I'm stricken with fear that you've forgotten me.
Sometimes I'm frightened that your loving heart
May have hardened against me through being misled
By what some spiteful gossip may have said.
And sometimes I fear a mishap on the way
Has turned my lover from his true intent
By some adversity or accident.
May God turn all such evil signs away!

MARY KNEW how important it was for Bothwell to spend his time assembling military forces to support her cause. All the same, her anxiety seems to have increased her physical need for him. When he failed to turn up one night as promised, she sat down and confronted on paper all her doubts and fears.

By now, the desire to prove her love had been overwhelmed by the terror, both irrational and horribly rational, that she could feel closing in on her mind. On 13 June 1567, she went to join Bothwell in Dunbar.

Ne vous voyant selon qu'avez promis,
J'ai mis la main au papier pour écrire
D'un différent que je voulus transcrire.
Je ne sais pas quel sera votre avis,
Mais je sais bien qui mieux aimer saura.
Vous direz bien qui plus y gagnera.

THIS SONNET stops short. Lines five and six make an unlikely place for a couplet in a sonnet. They were probably intended as the central lines for a more regular quatrain. At any rate, Mary never had the chance to finish it.

On 15 June at Carberry Hill in East Lothian, Bothwell and Mary rode at the head of an army to meet the massed forces of a confederation of Scottish nobles led by Morton, Home, Atholl, Mar, Glencairn, Lindsay, Ruthven and Kirkcaldy. After hours of parley, it was agreed that there should be no battle, but that the queen should return to Edinburgh without Bothwell.

Bothwell was given a safe conduct and fled to Norway, only to fall into the hands of a relative of his former mistress, Anna Throndsen. This was Erik Rosencrantz, one of the few real-life characters in Shakespeare's Hamlet. *Bothwell was imprisoned in Denmark. He died chained to a pillar in Dragsholm Castle eleven years later in April 1578. By a bizarre coincidence, one of the witnesses to his final confession was Morgens Guildenstern, Rosencrantz's diplomatic partner in* Hamlet.

Mary was taken from Carberry Hill to Edinburgh and locked up in the Black Turnpike in the High Street. The following day, 16 June

12.

Not seeing you, although you promised me,
I've taken pen and paper so to write
About a dispute that I would indite.
I do not know what your judgement may be,
But I know well which one of us loves best.
You'll clearly tell which one shall gain the most.

1567, she was seen leaning from a window half-naked and dishevelled screaming that she had been betrayed. She was imprisoned in the fortress on an island in Loch Leven where, in mid-July, her pregnancy ended in miscarriage or abortion.

Mary was twenty-four years old, Bothwell was thirty one. They never saw one another again.

Sir Francis Walsingham, the head of Queen Elizabeth's secret service. Portrait by J de Critz.

CHAPTER THREE

Early Years in Prison

AFTER MARY'S SURRENDER AT CARBERRY HILL, the rebel lords of Scotland imprisoned her in the island fortress of Lochleven Castle. Her jailer was Sir William Douglas, whose household included his mother, Lady Margaret, the mother of the bastard Earl of Moray by Mary's own father, James V.

Exhausted and distraught, Mary miscarried in July 1567. She had been bearing twins. Unlike many of the Stewarts, Prince James would have no sibling rivals.

Who was to rule Scotland now? The rebels chose Moray as Regent. Mary was forced to sign papers abdicating the throne of Scotland to the infant Prince James, placing him in Moray's protection. In Lochleven Castle, Lady Margaret gloated as her bastard son supplanted his legitimate half-sister.

The childless Queen Elizabeth I of England, godmother to Prince James, asked her envoy Nicholas Throckmorton to see if he could arrange for the prince

Opposite: *Queen Elizabeth I of England in 1558. Portrait by G Gower.*

to be brought up in England, promising 'we shall not fail but to yield as good safety for her son as can be devised for any that might be our child born of our own body'. His godfather, the French King Charles IX, wanted James to be brought up in France just as Mary had been. The Scottish nobles, however, would not let the prince out of their hands. They even appointed as his tutor George Buchanan, the same man who had compiled and manufactured evidence against Mary in his 'Detection'. Buchanan poisoned James's mind against his mother.

On 25 March 1568, Mary escaped from Lochleven Castle with the help of her jailer's brother George Douglas and his orphaned cousin Willie who dropped his handkerchief over the jailer's keys while handing him a drink. Willie picked up handkerchief and keys and escaped with the queen in a rowing boat.

Mary rallied an army but when she confronted the forces of Moray and Morton at Langside on 13 May, her troops were routed. She fled across the Solway to England where she was taken to Carlisle Castle and, as she wrote to the Earl of Cassilis, was 'right well and honourably treated'.

Queen Elizabeth saw Mary as a dangerous embarrassment, a rival for the throne of England and the focus of Catholic plots. Mary's status changed from unwanted guest to prisoner. Mary half believed that if she and

Elizabeth could meet in person their differences would be resolved and half that the opposite would happen and Elizabeth would condemn her to death.

What was this twenty-five-year-old captive queen like in these early years in England? Sir Francis Knollys, her jailer, was impressed:

'This lady and princess is a notable woman. She seemeth to regard no ceremonious honour beside the acknowledging of her estate regal. She showeth a disposition to speak much, to be bold, to be pleasant and to be very familiar. She showeth a great desire to be avenged of her enemies. She showeth a readiness to expose herself to all perils in hope of victory. She delighteth much to hear of hardiness and valiancy, commending by name all approved hardy men of her country, although they be her enemies, and she commendeth no cowardness even in her friends.'

In May 1568, Mary was moved to Bolton Castle. On 11 January 1570, the Earl of Moray was shot dead by an assassin. His replacement as Regent was the Earl of Lennox, father of Mary's murdered husband Darnley, but he too was killed within the year and was succeeded by the Earl of Morton. Mary was no closer to regaining her throne. For the next twenty years she was transferred from one stronghold to another in the north and midlands of England.

Sonnet à la Reine Elizabeth I d'Angleterre.

Un seul penser qui me profite et nuit,
Amer et doux, change en mon coeur sans cesse;
Entre le doute et l'espoir il m'oppresse
Tant que la paix et le repos me fuient.
Donc, chère soeur, si cette carte suit
L'affection de vous voir qui me presse,
C'est que je vis en peine et en tristesse
Si promptement l'effet ne s'en ensuit.
J'ai vu la nef relâcher par contrainte
En haute mer proche d'entrer au port
Et le serein se convertir en trouble.
Ainsi je suis en souci et en crainte,
Non pas de vous mais quant aux fois à tort* **où (manque)*
Fortune rompe voile et cordage double.

MARY GREW OBSESSED *with justifying her actions to Elizabeth. She wrote this poem, hoping to ease relations between them.*

Elizabeth's response was a hostile poem, printed in Puttenham's Arte of Englishe Poesie 1589 *in which she says:*

'No forreine bannisht wight shall ancre in this port,
Our realme it brookes no stranger's force, let them
elsewhere resort'.

William Cecil, Lord Burghley, Queen Elizabeth I's Secretary of State, who led the prosecution at Mary's trial. Att. to A Bronckhorst c. 1565.

Sonetto alla Regina Elizabetha I d'Inghlaterra.

Il pensier che mi nuoce insieme e giova,
Amaro et dolce al mio cor cangia spesso,
E fra tema e speranza lo tien 'si oppresso
Che la quiette pace unque non trouva.
Pero se questa carta a voi renuova
Il bel desio di vedervi in me impresso
Cio fa il grand affano ch'me se stesso
Ha non puotendo homai da se far proua.
Ho veduto talhor vicino al porto
Respinger naue in mer contrario uento;
E nel maggior seren' turbarsi il cielo:
Con Sorella chara, temo e pauento
Non gia per uoi, ma quanta volte a torto
Rompere fortuna un ben' ordito uello.

IN MAY 1570, Pope Pius V, in his bull 'Regnans in Excelsis', excommunicated Elizabeth and declared that her subjects no longer owed her any loyalty.

Roberto Ridolfi, an Italian banker, plotted to marry Mary to the Earl of Norfolk who would lead a Catholic coup in England. The plot failed. Norfolk was executed for high treason in June 1572 and many leading Catholics were jailed. It is ironic that Mary should have written her sonnet to Elizabeth in both French and Italian.

Sonnet to Queen Elizabeth I of England. *1568*

One thought, that is my torment and delight,
Ebbs and flows bittersweet within my heart
And between doubt and hope rends me apart
While peace and all tranquility take flight.
Therefore, dear sister, should this letter dwell
Upon my weighty need of seeing you,
It is that grief and pain shall be my due
Unless my wait should end both swift and well.
I've seen a ship's sails slackened by taut ropes
On the high tide at the harbour bar
And a clear sky suddenly fill with cloud;
Likewise fear and distress fill all my hopes,
Not because of you, but for the times there are
When Fortune doubly strikes on sail and shroud.

Mary's half-brother, James Stewart, Earl of Moray. Portrait by an unknown artist around 1568 when he was Regent of Scotland.

Méditation sur l'inconstance et vanité du monde, composée par la reine d'Ecosse et douairière de France, après avoir lu en prison les Consolationes *en latin, à elle envoyées par le St Evêque de Rosse.*

Lorsqu'il convient à chacun reposer
Et pour un temps tout souci déposer,
Un souvenir de mon amère vie
Me vient ôter de tout dormir l'envie,
Représentant à mes yeux vivement
De bien en mal un soudain changement,
Que distiller me fait lors sur la face
La triste humeur que tout plaisir efface;

JOHN LESLIE, BISHOP OF ROSS, *Mary's special envoy to Elizabeth, was jailed after the Ridolfi plot. Ross was a Catholic counterpart of George Buchanan, scholarly, ambitious and devious, but he lacked Buchanan's cool head and instinct for self-preservation.*

In prison, Ross composed a long treatise, Piae Afflicti Animi Consolationes Divinique Remedia, *intended to comfort Mary in her own prison. When she received it, Mary turned again to writing poetry to help come to terms with her situation.*

Much of what she says is orthodox piety. In the middle of the poem, however, she tries to reconcile the Protestant doctrine of salvation by predestination (i.e., from the moment you are born, God has already

Meditation on the Inconstancy and Vanity of the World, Composed by the Queen of Scotland and Dowager of France, after having read in prison the *Consolationes* in Latin sent to her by the Bishop of Ross. *1573*

When it is meet for rest to be our guide
And for a while set every care aside,
A memory of my bitter life doth creep
And robs my heart of all desire to sleep,
Holding an image clear before my face
Of good and evil swiftly changing place,
Whose burden brings into my eyes
A mood of sadness and all pleasure flies;

decided whether he wants you in heaven) and the Catholic doctrine of salvation by good works (i.e., heaven is your reward for observing the law of God during your lifetime on earth). It was one of the great religious debates of the day and Mary shows far greater tolerance and humility than her Calvinist political enemies, notably John Knox.

The poem is exactly one hundred lines long. Symbolic numerology was fashionable in Mary's day and she loved wordgames. She was no doubt well aware of how the numerology of this poem symbolized the revelation to men of spiritual essence and supreme power. It also represents the active principle which, broken in pieces, becomes multiplicity, appropriate in her case.

Dont tôt après, cherchant de m'alléger,
J'entre en discours, non frivole ou léger,
Considérant du monde l'inconstance
Et des mortels le trop peu d'assurance;
Jugeant par là rien n'être permanent
Ni bien ni mal dessous le firmament,
Ce qui soudain me met en souvenance
*Des sages dits du roi, pleins de prudence** **les maximes de Salomon*
J'ai (se dit-il) cherché tous les plaisirs
Qui peuvent plus assouvir mes désirs,
Mais je n'ai vu en cette masse ronde
Que vanité, donc fol est qui s'y fonde,
De quoi mes yeux expérience ont eu
Durant nos jours, car j'ai souvent vu
Ceux qui touchent les hauts cieux de la tête
Soudainement renversés par tempête.
Les plus grands rois, monarques, empereurs,
De leurs états et vies ne sont sûrs.
*Bâtir palais et amasser chevance** **richesse*
Retourne en bref en perte et décadence.
Etre venu de parents généreux
N'empêche point qu'on ne soit malheureux.
Les beaux habits, le jeu, le ris, la danse,
Ne laissent d'eux que deuil et repentance.
Et la beauté, tant agréable aux yeux,
Se part de nous quand nous devenons vieux.* **nous quitte*

Then afterwards, to lighten my despond,
I enter discourse, not on shallow ground,
Considering the world's inconstancy
And mortals' lack of true security;
Judging by that nothing is permanent
Nor good, nor bad beneath the firmament,
Which suddenly sets me remembering
The words of wisdom of that prudent king*. *Soloman
I have (he said) sought out each pleasure's way
Which can no longer my desires allay:
But I have seen upon the earth's round ball
Naught but vanity, folly therewithal,
That I have witnessed where'er I have been
In our lifetime for I have often seen
Those who touch the heavens with their brow
Suddenly struck down when fierce storms blow.
The greatest monarch, emperor or king
Is not sure of rank, nor life nor anything.
To build a palace and store wealth away
So quickly turns into loss and decay.
Coming from a generous family
Does not prevent living unhappily.
Fine clothes and sport and dance and laughter
Leave only grieving and remorse thereafter;
And beauty, so delightful to behold,
Deserts us utterly as we grow old:

Mary, Queen of Scots, and her son, James VI, in 1583. James is shown aged seventeen with his mother. It is a piece of wishful thinking by an unknown artist. In fact, Mary saw her son for the last time when he was only one year old.

Right: *The Conference Between Queen Mary and John Knox at Holyrood Palace in 1561. The painting shows Mary, who had just announced a royal policy of religious tolerance, confronted by the fanatical Protestant reformer, John Knox. The Catholic Mary is holding her rosary beads and has just laid down a piece of her famous embroidery. Knox is clutching the bible as if it were his personal property. A Victorian historical drama painting by Robert Herdman in 1875.*

Boire et manger et vivre tout à l'aise
Revient aussi à douleur et malaise.
Beaucoup d'amis, richesse, ni savoir,
De contenter, qui les a, n'ont pouvoir.
Bref, tout le bien de cette vie humaine
Se garde peu et s'acquiert à grande peine:
Que nous sert donc ici nous amuser
Aux vanités qui ne font qu'abuser?
Il faut chercher en bien plus haute place
Le vrai repos, le plaisir et la grâce,
Qui promis est à ceux qui de bon coeur
Retourneront à l'unique Sauveur;
Car au ciel est notre éternel partage
Jà ordonné pour nous en héritage.* *déjà
Mais qui pourra, O Père très humain,
Avoir cet heur, si tu n'y mets la main,* *bonheur
D'abondonner son péché et offense
En ayant fait condigne pénitence?* *digne
*Ou qui pourra ce monde dépriser** *déprécier
Pour seul t'aimer honorer et priser?
Nul pour certain si ta douce clémence,* *personne
Le prévenant, à tel bien ne l'avance.
Par quoi, Seigneur et Père Souverain,
Regarde-moi de ton visage serein,
Dont regardas la femme pécheresse
Qui à tes pieds pleuvait ses maux sans cesse;

To live at ease and eat and drink our fill
Leads also to more suffering and ill:
Great wealth and wisdom, many friends beside,
Is no sure way of being satisfied.
In short, all worldly goods in human life
Are quickly lost, and gained by bitter strife:
How doth it serve our purpose to believe
In vanities that flatter to deceive?
We must attempt to seek a higher place
For true repose, for pleasure and for grace.
Where those who, pure of heart, find their reward
When they return to the true Saviour Lord;
For our eternal lot awaits in heaven,
Preordained, a birthright to us given.
But which of us, O kindest Father, still
Can claim this fortune, save it be thy will
That he abandon sin and all offence
By having made a worthy penitence?
Who can renounce the world upon his own
To honour, love and cleave to thee alone?
None for sure unless thy tender mercy come
To warn and guide him to thy heavenly home;
Therefore, O almighty Father and Lord,
Look upon me with thy benign regard
As you looked on that woman full of sin
Who at thy feet poured out her ceaseless pain;

Dont regardas Pierre pareillement
Qui jà t'avait nié par jurement.* *déjà
Et comme à eux donne-moi cette grâce
Que ta merci tous mes péchés efface.* *ton pardon
En retirant de ce monde mon coeur
Fais l'aspirer à l'éternel bonheur.
Donne, Seigneur, donne-moi patience,
Amour et foi et en Toi espérance,
L'humilité, avec dévotion,
De te servir de pure affection.
Envois-moi ta divine prudence
Pour empêcher que péché ne m'offense.
Jamais de moi n'éloigne vérité,
Simple douceur avec charité,
La chasteté et la persévérance.
Demeure en moi avec obéissance.

James, Earl of Morton, painted by an unknown artist around 1577 when he was Regent of Scotland.

As you looked upon Peter just the same,
He who already had forsworn thy name.
And, as to them, grant me thy grace I pray
So that thy mercy wash my sins away.
In taking my heart from a world like this,
I'll seek to make it win eternal bliss.
Grant, O Lord, your patience unto me,
With love and faith and always trust in thee.
Grant me devotion and humility
With pure intent to serve you loyally:
Send me your prudence that I may remain
Free from sinfulness and mortal stain.
Never take thy truth away from me,
Fill me with meekness and with charity:
Let chastity and perseverance
Live in my heart with all obedience.

John Leslie, Bishop of Ross, Mary's most influential Catholic churchman. Portrait by an unknown artist.

De toutes erreurs, Seigneur, préserve-moi
Et tous les jours, Christ, augmente la foi
Que j'ai reçue de ma Mère, l'Eglise
Ou j'ai recours pour mon lieu de franchise
Contre péché, ignorance et orgueil,
Qui font aller au perdurable deuil.* **perpétuel*
Permets, Seigneur que toujours mon bon Ange
Soit près de moi et t'offre ma louange,
Mes oraisons, mes larmes et soupirs
Et de mon coeur tous justes désirs.
**Ton Saint esprit sur ma face demeure,* **que (manque)*
Tant que voudras qu'en ce monde je dure.
Et quand, Seigneur, de clémence et bonté
M'ôter voudras de la captivité
Où mon esprit réside en cette vie,
Pleine de maux, de tourments et d'ennuis,
Me souvenir donne-moi le pouvoir
De tes mercis et fiance** y avoir* **pardons* ***foi*
Ayant au coeur ta passion écrite
Que offrirai au lieu de mon mérite.
Donc, mon Dieu, ne m'abondonne point,
Et mêmement en cet extrême point
A seule fin que tes voies je tienne,
Et que vers toi à la fin je parvienne.

Sa vertue m'attire. (*Anagramme de son nom*)

Marie Stuvarte.

From every error, Lord, protect my path,
And every day, O Christ, protect the faith
That my mother Church has given me
Where I withdraw to let myself be free
From sin and ignorance and pride,
The road where everlasting woes abide.
Grant, Lord, that my guardian Angel always
Be close to me and offer you my praise,
My prayers, my tears, my sighs, so to impart
All the just desires of my heart.
May thy Holy Spirit shine on me always
While you will me to live out my earthly days.
And when, Lord, in your bounteous clemency
You wish to free me from captivity,
Where my spirit has its dwelling in this life,
Full of sorrows, torments and of strife,
Remember me and grant to me, I pray,
Thy mercy's power and trust in it alway,
My love for you engraved upon my heart,
An offering to replace my just desert.
Therefore, my God, do not forsake me now,
And when I reach my final end also,
Following in thy paths, grant that it be my due
That at the last I draw near unto you.

I am drawn to his virtue. (*French anagram of Marie Stuvarte*)

Mary Stewart

Sonnet écrit quand elle était prisonnière.

L'ire de Dieu par le sang ne s' apaise
De boeufs, ni boucs, épandus sur l'autel;
Ni par encens ou sacrifice tel
Le souverain ne reçoit aucune aise.
**Qui veut, Seigneur, faire oeuvre qui te plaise* **Celui (manque)*
Il faut qu'il ait sa foi en l'Immortel
Avec espoir, charité aux mortels
*Et bien faisant que tes lois il ne taise.** **ignore*
L'oblation qui t'est seule agréable
C'est un esprit en oraison constant,
Humble et dévot en un corps chaste étant.
O Tout-Puissant, sois-moi si favorable
Que pour toujours ces grâces dans mon coeur
Puissent rester à ta gloire et honneur.

Va, tu meriteras. *(Anagramme de Marie Stuvarte)*

THE POEM WAS PUBLISHED IN *1574 in the first edition of the* Consolationes *by the Bishop of Ross. Its rejection of the fancy trappings of religion would have pleased Mary's arch-enemy John Knox, but her belief in the doctrine of good works is opposite to the rigid Calvinist doctrine of predestination.*

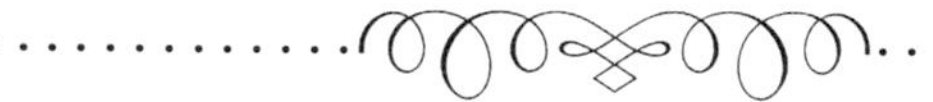

Sonnet Written During Her Imprisonment.

The wrath of God is not appeased by blood
Of goats nor oxen on the altar laid;
No incense nor any sacrifice made
Brings satisfaction to the Lord our God.
Those who seek to please you must maintain,
O Lord, their faith in immortality
And to mankind bear hope and charity
And do good works, nor take thy laws in vain.
The only offering that pleases you
Is a mind that dwells in constant prayer
In a living chaste body, devout and humble there.
Almighty God, grant that it be my due
To bear these gifts in my heart all my days
And offer them to your eternal praise.

Go now. You are worthy. *(French anagram of Marie Stuvarte)*

The little envoi, sending the poem on its way, is very much in the tradition of the Latin authors whom Mary read and liked. 'Va, tu meriteras' is also an anagram of 'Marie Stuveart', another play on her name.

A l'Evêque de Ross, après sa délivrance de prison.

Puisque Dieu a, par sa bonté immense,
Permis qu'ayez obtint tant de bonheur* **obtenu*
De départir en crédit et faveur
Hors de prison, en saine conscience,

Remerciez sa divine clémence,
Qui de tous biens est seul cause et auteur,
Et le priez, d'un humble et dévot coeur,
Qu'il ait pitié de ma longue souffrance.

Sa vertue m'attire. *(Anagramme de Marie Stuvarte)*

THIS POEM IS NOT AMONG *those printed in the first edition of Bishop Leslie's* Consolationes, *but it appears in a later French edition of 1595. It must have been written just too late for the 1574 edition when the bishop was newly released from prison.*

After his implication in the Norfolk conspiracy, Ross was committed to the custody of the Bishop of London, who begged to have him removed to the Bishop of Winchester, who in turn prayed 'to be delivered from the Bishop of Ross'. His quick temper and lack of tact, allied to his great erudition and love of arguing, made him a wearying member of any household.

The phrase 'humble et dévot' occurs in Mary's previous poem 'L'Ire de Dieu' and was a theme that preoccupied her for the rest of her life.

To the Bishop of Ross, After His Deliverance from Prison. *1574*

Since God has, in his generosity,
Granted you such good fortune now
In all good standing to be free to go,
With a clear conscience, from captivity,

Give thanks for his heavenly clemency
Which is the source and cause of all accord,
And with a humble heart pray to the Lord
That in my long ordeal he pity me.

I am drawn to his virtue. *(French anagram of Marie Stuvarte)*

King James VI as a young man, shown with the royal arms of Scotland. Engraving by R.E.

CHANANVS ORA SIC VVLTVM TVLIT
CRIPTA ET ASTRA NOOSSE SI MENTEM
TIS. 76.

CHAPTER FOUR

What I Was I No More Remain

Over the next few years, Mary was moved from prison to prison: from damp, draughty Tutbury Castle in Staffordshire to Chatsworth, Sheffield Castle and Wingfield in Derbyshire. Her jailer was the Earl of Shrewsbury, a kindly, hard-working man with a powerful sense of duty. He had made an unfortunate marriage to Bess of Hardwicke, a grasping, spiteful woman whose selfishness, ill-temper and treachery became a torment to her husband. Life in their household was tense and unpleasant.

Shrewsbury enjoyed Mary's company, though he complained about the cost of keeping her. Mary's retinue for most of her imprisonment contained between thirty and forty servants and officials. When Elizabeth first gave Mary to Shrewsbury to guard in 1569, he was allowed

Opposite: *George Buchanan. Classical poet and political opportunist who compiled and fabricated evidence against Mary. Portrait by an unknown artist.*

£52 each week to maintain her household. In 1575, this was cut to £30 a week. Shrewsbury complained, but the notoriously stingy Elizabeth told him to bear the extra cost himself, implying that he would fall from favour if he did not. He spent an estimated £10,000 each year of his own money on his royal prisoner. Even for such a rich man, it was a ruinous expense.

Bess of Hardwicke sought to ingratiate herself with Mary. The two women loved needlework and spent hours together working on embroideries, many of which survive today. Mary's wordgames show as much in her embroidery as in her poetry. She made anagrams of her name, Marie Stuart, like 'Sa vertue m'attire' (I am drawn to his/her virtue), and adopted the motto 'En ma fin est mon commencement' (In my end is my beginning).

Mary's health began to fail. She had rheumatism in her legs which gave her a limp. From early childhood, she had loved exercise, particularly riding and dancing. Now, locked up in damp castles, she began to put on weight. She had a nagging pain in her side which sometimes became so intense that she fainted. At other times, her stomach could not keep food down and she became dangerously weak. At first her jailers thought she was faking, but her symptoms were all too real.

Locked in prison, it was hard for Mary to have a picture of the political realities outside. In 1581, she

learned that the Regent Morton had been executed, allegedly for his part in the murder of Darnley fourteen years before. Mary stood accused of the same crime, though she had never been allowed to see the evidence compiled and manufactured against her. Her son James was now fourteen and had been well trained by his tutor Buchanan in the ways of political trickery. Mary wondered how he felt about the mother of whom he had no memory. His polite, business letters gave her no hint of his feelings.

Mary had little to do but let her mind churn over her fate. She poured out letters to Elizabeth, to relatives in France and friends at home and abroad, all with the same theme – that she sought no more than an end to her captivity and the right to reclaim the throne of Scotland. In more private letters, she still saw herself as the head of the Catholic cause in Britain.

One of her most treasured possessions was the Book of Hours that had been a gift from the Dauphin Francis before they were married. It was a poignant memento of the time when she had been the most dazzling princess in the most sophisticated court in Europe. In prison, Mary began to write little verses in its margins. Many are dense and ambiguous, matters between her and God, not intended for any other reader. Her mind was already turning from this world to the next.

Versets écrits dans son livre d'heures.

Qui jamais davantage eut contraire le sort?
Si la vie n'est moins utile que la mort.* *Ainsi
*Et plutôt que changer de mes maux l'aventure** *le cours
Chacun change pour moi d'humeur et de nature.

Fe*: Marie R. **Fait par*

Comme autres fois la renommée
Ne vole plus par l'univers
Ici borne son cours divers
La chose d'elle plus aimée.

Marie R.

Mary, Queen of Scots at Fotheringhay. Mary is seen tranquilly contemplating her fate while her attendants are stricken with grief and horror. A Symbolist documentary painting by John Duncan in 1929.

Verses Written in Her Book of Hours. *1579*

Did any more ill-fated e'er draw breath?
Wherefore life has no more use than death.
Rather than change my sorrows' destiny,
All change their mood and manner unto me.

Written by: Queen Mary.

My fame, unlike in former days,
No longer flies from coast to coast.
And what confines her wandering ways?
– The very thing she loves the most.

Queen Mary.

MARY'S HANDWRITING IN THESE verses is unsteady and almost elderly, a broken version of her earlier neat courtly hand. She also seems to have had problems with her quill pens; one is scratchy and another makes blots.

Several of these verses are rebuses, punning wordgames which let her play on the notion of 'heur' meaning both 'hour' and 'good fortune'. In the second one, she shows the paradox of prison giving her the chance to achieve the only fame she truly values – a reputation for being devout.

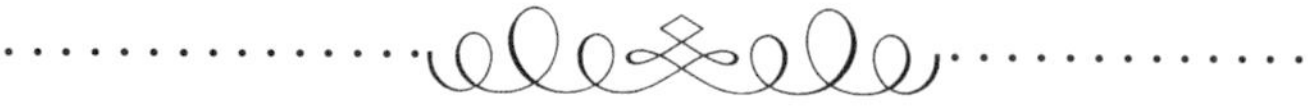

Les heures je guide et le jour
Par l'ordre de ma carrière,
Quittant mon triste séjour
Pour ici croître ma lumière.

◆

Celle que d'honneur sait combler
Chacun, du bruit de sa louange,
Ne peut moins qu'à soi ressembler
En effet n'étant qu'un bel ange.

◆

Il n'appartient porter ces armes
Qu'à ceux qui, d'un coeur indompté
Comme nous, n'ont peur des alarmes
Du temps puissant mais sans bonté.

IN THE TOP VERSE, Mary speaks in two voices. In the voice of her Book of Hours, she talks about the pattern of religious devotion. In her own voice, she says that, although her devotions are a source of comfort, her daily routine is so predictable that others can tell the time by her!

Mary's use of 'R' after her signature in some of these poems shows how conscious she was of being a queen, even in prison.

Mary's Book of Hours was put in a new binding long after her death. The pages were trimmed to reduce the margins and half of the poem on p. 90 beginning 'Il faut plus que la renommée' has been lost.

I guide the hours and guide the day
Because my course is true and right
And thus I quit my own sad stay
That here I may increase my light.

Since she makes honour her mainstay,
Each, who with flattery doth blare,
Falls short of her likeness alway,
Being in truth an angel fair.

None has the right to bear these arms
But those whose dauntless hearts withstood,
Like us, the terror of alarms
In powerful times devoid of good.

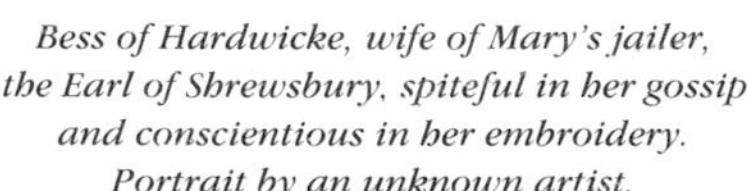

Bess of Hardwicke, wife of Mary's jailer, the Earl of Shrewsbury, spiteful in her gossip and conscientious in her embroidery. Portrait by an unknown artist.

MARY WORKED AT THESE *little verses in several variations. The image of a guardian angel figures prominently. She takes spiritual comfort from it and tries to identify with it as if she still saw herself as the true material guardian of her kingdom.*

*Un coeur, que l'outrage martyre** *martyrise
Par un mépris ou d'un refus,
A le pouvoir de faire dire:
Je ne suis plus ce que je fus.

Marie

Si nos pensers sont élevés
Ne l'estimez pas chose étrange.
Ils méritent être approuvés,
Ayant pour objet un bel ange.

◆

Pour récompense et pour salaire
De mon amour et de ma foi
Rendez, mon ange tutélaire;
Autant comme je vous en dois.

◆

En feinte mes amis changent leur bienveillance.
Tout le bien qu'ils me font est désirer ma mort,
Et comme si, mourant, j'étais en défaillance
Dessus mes vêtements ils ont jeté le sort.

◆

Il faut plus que la renommée
Pour dire et publier . . .

A heart which suffers agony
Through scorn, rejection and disdain
Still has the power and right to say:
'What I was I no more remain'.

Mary

George Talbot, Sixth Earl of Shrewsbury, Mary's jailer for many years, who generally treated her as well as he could. Portrait by an unknown artist.

If our thoughts rise heavenward
Do not think it strange or rare.
They should be held in high regard
For they behold an angel fair.

◆

For the reward and salary
That my love and faith are due,
My guardian angel, give to me
Just as much as I owe you.

◆

With feigned good will my friends change toward me,
All the good they do me is to wish me dead,
As if, while I lay dying helplessly,
They cast lots for my garments round my bed.

◆

Never again in all my fame must I
Proclaim and tell . . .

Bien plus utile est l'heure que non pas la fortune
Puisqu'elle change autant qu'elle est opportune.

◆

La vieillesse est un mal qui ne se peut guérir
Et la jeunesse un bien qui pas un ne ménage,
Qui fait qu'aussitôt né l'homme est près de mourir,
Et qui l'on croit heureux travaille davantage.

Versets. *1582*

Celui vraiment n'a point de courtoisie
Qui en bon lieu ne montre son savoir;
Etant requis d'écrire en poésie,
Il vaudrait mieux du tout n'en point avoir.

◆

Les dieux, les cieux, la mort et la haine et l'envie
Sont sourds, irés, cruels, animés contre moi.* **furieux*
Prier, souffrir, pleurer, à chacun être amie,
Sont les remèdes seuls qu'en tant d'ennuis je vois.

Time is more use to us than wealth or fate
Because it changes when appropriate.

◆

Old age is an ill that none can cure
And youth a good that nobody can store.
As soon as man is born his death is sure
And those who seem happy merely struggle more.

erses. *1582*

A man is lacking in civility
If, when time calls, he fail to show his wit
And when the occasion merits poetry
He would far rather have no part of it.

◆

The gods, the heavens, death, envy and hate rail on;
They are deaf, angry, cruel, marshalled against me.
To pray, weep, suffer, be a friend to everyone
Are the only cures for the many woes I see.

THESE TWO VERSES WERE only recognized as being by Mary, Queen of Scots, three hundred years after her death when they were identified in the Public Record Office by Marham Thorpe while compiling the document calendars for Mary's period.

CHAPTER FIVE

Trial and Execution

MARY'S HEALTH CONTINUED to be poor. While she was a prisoner in Chatsworth, the Earl of Shrewsbury eventually allowed her to visit the nearby spa of Buxton Wells to take the waters. She was even permitted to go riding under close guard and to keep dogs and hawks which she exercised.

In 1582 Shrewsbury's son and heir Giles died and his marriage began to break up. His wife, Bess of Hardwicke, was intensely jealous of Mary and began to spread stories that Mary and Shrewsbury were lovers. Bess cold-bloodedly tried to discredit her husband in an effort to blackmail him into giving her a better divorce settlement. Both Mary and Shrewsbury were furious at this slur on their honour. Bess admitted to the English Council that the rumours were untrue, but she had already damaged their reputations.

Mary had by now been a prisoner for sixteen years. She

Opposite: *The Execution of Mary, Queen of Scots. Detail of a Romantic dramatic painting by Robert Herdman in 1867.*

was out of touch with the political realities of the new Europe and relied for information on letters that were often censored.

In 1583, Francis Throckmorton, a cousin of Elizabeth's envoy to Mary, Nicholas Throckmorton, was arrested and confessed to a plot between Mary, her French Guise relatives and the Earl of Northumberland to organize a Spanish invasion of England. Throckmorton was executed.

Elizabeth's Secretary of State, Lord Burghley, wanted Mary disposed of once and for all to put an end to Catholic plots. In January 1585, she was taken back to the dank Tutbury Castle and handed over to Sir Amyas Paulet, a jailer as grim and cold as the prison he kept.

In 1586 Sir Anthony Babington, a former page to Shrewsbury, tried to organize another plot to put Mary on the throne of England. The conspirators wrote to Mary, proposing that Elizabeth be assassinated. Mary replied, unaware that the correspondence was being monitored by Francis Walsingham, the head of Queen Elizabeth's secret service.

At last there was hard evidence that Mary was prepared to supplant Elizabeth. Mary was taken first to Chartley then to Fotheringhay Castle in Northamptonshire. On 15 October, English parliamentary commissioners found her guilty of conspiracy against Elizabeth.

The only possible sentence was death.

James VI of Scotland protested to Elizabeth, but not too hard, not wanting to compromise his position as heir to the throne of England. King Henry III of France pled for the life of his brother Francis II's widow but without success.

Elizabeth was reluctant to sign the death warrant, knowing that to authorize the execution of a monarch could set a dangerous precedent for herself. Months passed, during which Mary never knew when she might find herself dragged from her apartments in Fotheringhay and put on the block. Eventually, Walsingham persuaded Elizabeth to sign the warrant on 1 February 1587.

On the evening of Tuesday 7 February, Mary was told she was to be executed the following morning at eight o'clock. She wrote a poem tranquilly accepting her fate. Her last lines were:

> 'Being punished in a world like this
> I've earned my portion in eternal bliss.'

When she was less than a week old, Mary inherited the crown of Scotland. At the age of sixteen she became queen of France. By the age of twenty-four she had lost three husbands and was to spend the next twenty years as a prisoner. At the age of forty-four she was dead.

O Seigneur Dieu, recevez ma prière.

O Seigneur Dieu, recevez ma prière
Qui est selon ta sainte volonté,
Car s'il ne plaît à ta grande majesté
Je te défendrai à la dernière carrière.
Hélas, Seigneur, je retourne en arrière;
Lasse déjà si ta grande bonté
Ne renforce ma frêle volonté
De ta vertu à franchir la barrière.
Tu veux, Seigneur, être maître du coeur.
Viens donc, Seigneur, et fais ta demeure
Pour en chasser l'amour et la rancoeur,
Le bien, le mal, m'ôtant tout souci,
Fors seulement de parvenir à Toi,
Pénitament et constante en ma foi.* **pénitente*

Sir Amyas Paulet, Mary's final jailer. Portrait by an unknown artist.

O Lord My God, Receive My Prayer. *1583*

O Lord my God, receive my prayer
Which is according to thy holy will;
For if, O great king, it should please thee still
I shall defend thee while I still draw air.
Alas, O Lord, I shall backslide once more,
Fatigued too soon unless thy bounty fill
And give resolve unto my own weak will
And with thy virtue open wide the door.
You wish, Lord, to be master of my heart.
Come then O Lord and make me your redoubt
That earthly love and hate be driven out
And good and evil and all care depart.
Only allow me to draw near to you,
Repentant, constant in my faith and true.

MARY CROWDED THIS SONNET *and the next one on to a small sheet of paper with her poem to Ronsard. The manuscript shows she had great difficulty finding words to confront with total honesty the weaknesses she saw within herself: lack of willpower, vulnerability to both love and rancour, recklessness and wavering faith.*

Donne, Seigneur, donne-moi patience.

Donne, Seigneur, donne-moi patience
Et renforce ma trop débile foi.
Que ton esprit me conduise en ta loi
Et me garde de choir par imprudence.
Donne, Seigneur, donne-moi la constance
En bien et mal la persévérance.
Reluis en Toi toute mon espérance
Et hors du coeur m'ôte tout vain émoi.
Ne permet qu'au monde je n'abuse
Mais tout plaisir fors en Toi je refuse.
Délivre-moi de toutes passions,
D'ire, d'erreur et de tout autre vice,
Et prouve-moi de douleur et justice* **éprouve*
D'un coeur dévot et bonnes actions.

Give Me, O Lord, the Patience to Progress. *1583*

Give me, O Lord, the patience to progress
And give resolve to my too feeble faith.
May thy spirit guide me in thy holy path
And shield me from all lapse and recklessness.
Give me, O Lord, the courage I require
In good and ill and perseverance too.
Rekindle all my hope and trust in you
And cleanse my heart of every vain desire.
Keep me from trespass and duplicity,
Forsaking every pleasure save in thee.
Deliver me from every false passion,
From anger, delusion and all wrongdoing;
Let me bear witness through the suffering
Of a faithful heart and deeds well done.

EVEN WHEN SHE IS addressing God, Mary cannot resist a pun. In the last verse 'passions' has its usual meaning of physical emotions, but in this religious context it also implies Christ's passion, his agony when he was executed on the cross.

As she struggled to clarify her thoughts, Mary scored out lines and altered rhymes. It was only with the help of new ultra-violet technology that I was able to reconstruct this sonnet and the previous one.

Versets à Ronsard.

Ronsard, si ton bon coeur de gentille nature
Te ment pour le respect d'un peu de nourriture
Qu'en tes plus jeunes ans tu as reçue d'un roi
De ton roi allié et de sa même loi,* *à ton roi

Je dirai non couard ni taché d'avarice* *te (manque)
Mais digne à mon avis du nom de brave prince.
Hélas! Ne scrivez pas ses faits ni ses grandeurs* *écrivez
Mais qu'il a bien voulu empêcher des malheurs.

IN 1583 RONSARD DEDICATED a volume of verse to Mary and sent her a sonnet in captivity. Mary found it impossible to write a good poem in reply. She wrote this poem on the same sheet of paper as her 'Prayer in Prison', with much erasing and scoring out.

After the second line in the second verse, she wrote and scored out

'Ou bien si tu as eu quelquefois le désir'
(Or if you sometimes have wished)

She found that she could only express in clichés and clumsy verse her compassion towards the old poet who was now in poor health. This must have been particularly frustrating for her, since she wanted to send a worthy poem to the man who had taught her the craft of verse.

Mary never finished the poem and instead sent Ronsard a casket containing two thousand crowns and a silver vase, with the device of Pegasus drinking at the fountain of Castalay at Mons Parnassus, inscribed 'A Ronsard – l'Apollo à la source des Muses'.

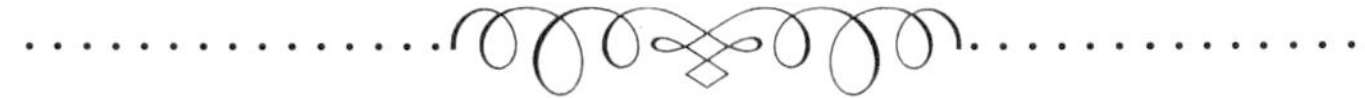

Verses to Ronsard. *1583*

Ronsard, if your good, gentle-natured heart
Deceives you for some sustenance at court,
Which you received when young from a king's hand
In harmony with the royal command,

No stain of greed nor cowardice shall I proclaim
But that you merit a brave prince's name.
Alas! Tell not of the heights to which he rose
But that he'd fain be succoured in his woes.

Pierre de Ronsard, the great French poet. Mary's literary mentor and friend throughout her life. Portrait by an unknown artist.

Écrit à la Station Thermale de Buxton Wells.

Buxtona, quae calidae celebrans nomen lymphae,
Fortuna mihi posthoc non adeunda, vale.

Poème composé le matin de son éxécution.

O Domine Deus speravi in Te.
O care mi Jesu nunc libera me.
In dura catena, in misera poena, desidero.
Languendo, gemendo, et genuflectendo,
Adoro, imploro, ut liberes me.

MARY OFTEN VISITED the spa at Buxton when she was in the charge of the Earl of Shrewsbury. When she wrote the couplet above, she knew that these outings for her health were about to stop and that she would be kept in close confinement.

Agnes Strickland tells us that Mary wrote the couplet on the window of her bedchamber in the Old Hall at Buxton but, 'This specimen of Mary Stuart's classical learning and genius was unfortunately destroyed about the middle of the last (i.e., eighteenth) century, in an

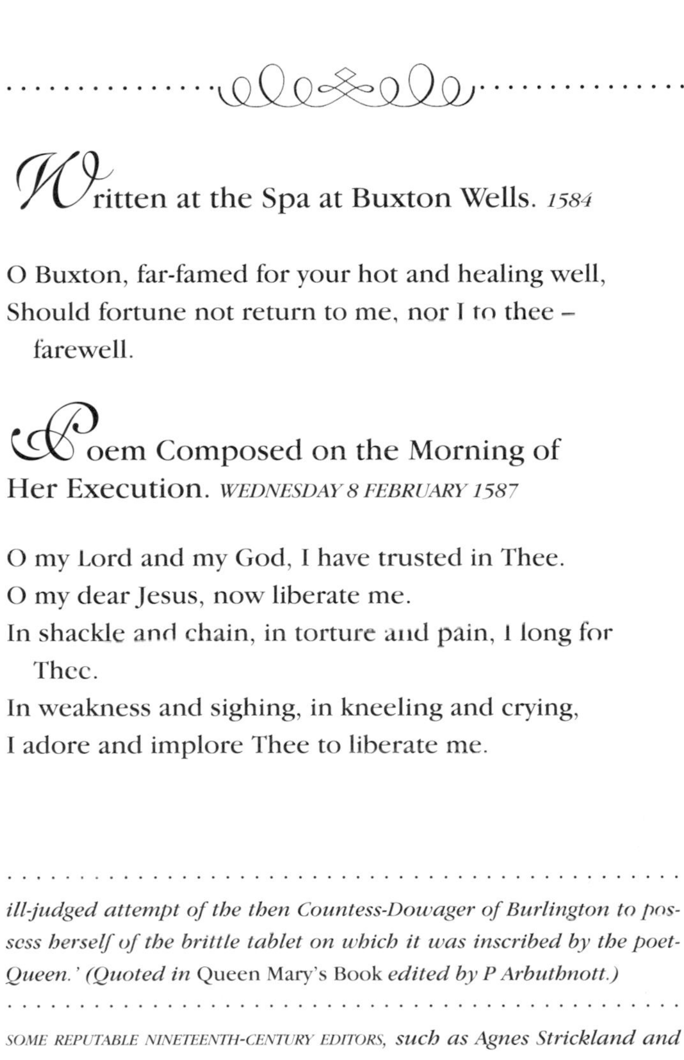

Written at the Spa at Buxton Wells. *1584*

O Buxton, far-famed for your hot and healing well,
Should fortune not return to me, nor I to thee –
farewell.

Poem Composed on the Morning of Her Execution. *WEDNESDAY 8 FEBRUARY 1587*

O my Lord and my God, I have trusted in Thee.
O my dear Jesus, now liberate me.
In shackle and chain, in torture and pain, I long for
Thee.
In weakness and sighing, in kneeling and crying,
I adore and implore Thee to liberate me.

ill-judged attempt of the then Countess-Dowager of Burlington to possess herself of the brittle tablet on which it was inscribed by the poet-Queen.' (Quoted in Queen Mary's Book *edited by P Arbuthnott.)*

SOME REPUTABLE NINETEENTH-CENTURY EDITORS, *such as Agnes Strickland and Julian Sharman, attribute 'O Domine Deus' to Mary without giving an original source. I am not convinced that it is authentic. The chiming Latin is unlike anything else she wrote.*

TODAY NOTHING IS LEFT OF *Fotheringhay Castle but a steep earthen mound covered with thistles and wild roses with a few cows grazing peacefully beside the river nearby.*

During her last days, Mary could hear the hammering of the carpenters as they built a scaffold. She kept looking out over the countryside, awaiting the arrival of the party of nobles who would supervise her execution. Myth has it that she etched a short poem with a diamond ring on her chamber window:

'From the top of all my trust
Mishap has laid me in the dust,'

but no evidence of that couplet survives and, if it is hers, it would be the first and last poem in English that she wrote.

Her final sonnet, written at Fotheringhay, is one of her greatest and most moving poems. The opening line is eerily like a poem written just a few miles from Fotheringhay over two hundred years later, John Clare's 'In Northampton County Asylum', which begins:

'I am, yet what I am, who cares or knows?'

By this time, Mary's handwriting is more even and steady than in the verses written eight years before in her Book of Hours. The end of the poem is similar to her 'Meditation' on the Bishop of Ross's Consolationes. *Her desire to earn her reward in heaven is unchanged, except that in this poem she knows she can now do no more to earn it.*

Her wry humour did not desert her even in her final tragedy. Line four contains a pun: 'mourir en vie'/'mourir envie' meaning: 'death in life'/'the desire to die'.

Opposite: *King James VI of Scotland after he had succeeded Elizabeth I to become King James I of England. Portrait by an unknown artist.*

Sonnet écrit au château de Fotheringhay.

Que suis-je hélas? Et de quoi sert ma vie?
Je ne suis fors qu'un corps privé de coeur,* *plus
Une ombre vaine, un objet de malheur
Qui n'a plus rien que de mourir en vie.* *jeu de mots: en vie/envie
Plus ne me portez, O ennemis, d'envie
A qui n'a plus l'esprit à la grandeur.
J'ai consommé d'excessive douleur
*Votre ire en bref de voir assouvie.** *apaisée
Et vous, amis, qui m'avez tenue chère,
Souvenez-vous que sans coeur et sans santé
Je ne saurais aucune bonne oeuvre faire,
Souhaitez donc fin de calamité
Et que, ici-bas étant assez punie,
J'aie ma part en la joie infinie.

MARY'S LAST LETTER, *written to her brother-in-law King Henry III of France on the eve of her execution, ends with these words:*

> *'I ask you to pay the wages due to my servants and to have prayers offered to God for a queen who has borne the title Most Christian, and who dies a catholic, stripped of all her possessions. As for my son, I commend him to you as far as he deserves, for I cannot answer for him . . .*
> *Wednesday, at two in the morning.*
> *Your most loving and most true sister.'*

Sonnet Written at Fotheringhay Castle. *1587*

Alas what am I? What use has my life?
I am but a body whose heart's torn away,
A vain shadow, an object of misery
Who has nothing left but death-in-life.
O my enemies, set your envy all aside;
I've no more eagerness for high domain;
I've borne too long the burden of my pain
To see your anger swiftly satisfied.
And you, my friends who have loved me so true,
Remember, lacking health and heart and peace,
There is nothing worthwhile I can do;
Ask only that my misery should cease
And that, being punished in a world like this,
I have my portion in eternal bliss.

pour vous me laisser de quoy fonder
& fayre les aulmosnes requises
edy a deulx heures apres minuict

Vostre tres affectionnee & bien
bonne soeur Marie R

ANNOTATED BIBLIOGRAPHY

The following chronological short list may help those who wish to find for themselves the earliest sources for Mary's poems:

Caligula BV fol 316. Cotton Collection. British Library. Ms. 1568.
Text of sonnet to Queen Elizabeth I in French and Italian.

Ane Detection Of The Duinges Of Marie, Quene Of Scottes, Touchand The Murder Of Hir Husband. 1571, 1573.
The Sonnets to Bothwell are included among other documents, letters and sworn statements assembled as evidence of Mary's complicity in the murder of Darnley. The Detection itself is an analysis by George Buchanan, heavily biased against her.

Piae Afflicti Animi Consolationes Divinaeque Remedia. John Leslie, Bishop of Ross. Paris. 1574, 1595.
Texts of 'Meditation on the Inconstancy and Vanity of the World', sent to the Bishop of Ross after reading his *Consolationes* and also 'L'ire de Dieu'. A further poem, 'To The Bishop Of Ross After His Deliverance From Prison', appears in the 1595 edition.

De Republica Anglorum Instauranda. Sir Thomas Chaloner. London 1579.
Latin text of 'The Diamond Speaks'. Translated, probably by Chaloner himself, from Mary's French poem which is now lost.

Tetrasticha, Ou Quatrains A Son Fils. Circa 1580.
This manuscript, also known as 'Institutions Of A Prince', was written by Mary for her son, James VI and I. I add it to the bibliography not because I have seen it, but because I have not. It was given by the poet William Drummond of Hawthornden to the library of the College of Edinburgh (now Edinburgh University) and seems to have gone missing some time in the seventeenth century. If it still exists in some private library, it would be of the greatest interest.

Mary's poem to her son may well have been an attempt to balance the rather strange education he received at the hands of George Buchanan. It would be fascinating to read what she had to say about how a monarch should behave. Her Italian reading would have made her aware of Machiavelli and Castiglione and her own contrasting experiences at the courts of France and Scotland, followed by her long imprisonment at the hands of another monarch, would have concentrated her mind wonderfully. She embroidered the cover of the manuscript herself and Bishop James Montague considered it 'a most pretious jewell'.

Mary, Queen of Scots. Vol XII. 31. Manuscript in Public Rec
approx.

Texts of 'Cela Vraiment N'a Poinct De Courtoisie' and also 'L
Cieux, La Mort'. First attributed to Mary by Marham Thorpe, who c
Record Office calendars for Mary's period.

Mary Stuart Archive Fc8 Nos 22-24. Manuscripts in Bodleian Library, C
1583, 1587 approx.

Texts of Sonnets in Prison I and II, Verses to Ronsard and Sonnet writte
Fotheringhay Castle.

Vita Mariae Stuartae Scotiae Reginae. Georgius Conaeus (George Conn). Rome. 1624. p61.

Latin translation, possibly by George Buchanan, of 'The Diamond Speaks', a poem whose original French text is lost. I used both Chaloner's (see above) and Conn's Latin versions for my English translation to give me the clearest idea of what Mary wrote in French.

Vie Des Dames Illustres. Pierre de Bourdeilles, Seigneur de Brantôme. Leyden. 1665.

Text of the ode on the death of Francis II.

De Vita Et Rebus Gestiis Serenissimae Principis Mariae Scotorum Reginae. Samuel Jebb. London 1725. Vol II pp 23-24.

Text of the ode on the death of Francis II.

Receuil Des Lettres, Instructions Et Memoires De Marie Stuart. Vol VII p 346-352. Ed. Prince Alexandre Labanoff. 1844.

Texts of verses written in Mary's Book of Hours, the original of which was preserved in the Imperial Library in St Petersburg until the Russian Revolution in 1917 and is now in the M E Saltykov-Schedrin Library in St Petersburg MS Lat Q. V.I. 112. Photographs of the relevant leaves in the Book of Hours exist in the Advocates' Library of the National Library of Scotland. MS 81.55.

The Poems of Mary, Queen of Scots. Ed. Julian Sharman. London. 1873.

Texts of several of Mary's poems, but with many omissions. He gives no sources for his texts. He includes the Latin poem from Buxton Wells. He also quotes the two line poem supposedly written on a window in Fotheringhay Castle.

Poésies Françaises de Marie Stuart. M Pawlowsi. In *Le Livre,* Paris. 1873.

This article includes the quatrain written in her aunt's prayer book and the poem to the Bishop of Ross on his release from prison.

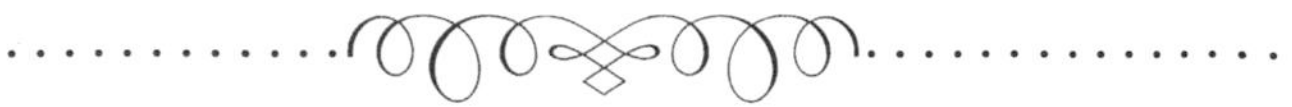

ondon. 1907.
'arly source book to date for Mary's 's, she includes a large number of Strickland. In her zeal for Mary's a mixture of Gothic romanticism ense for rhyme. To give Agnes translation attempted by later 'r.

arl of Bothwell. Ed. Joh Enschede en

onnets, including lines missing from the 'Detec- urteen of 'Elle Pour Son Honneur' and line six of 'Mon a fine-edition Christmas gift booklet with only 250 copies, the manuscript: VII.47.19 in the Cambridge University catalogue nuscripts.

The Silver Casket. Ed. Clifford Bax. London. 1946.
Texts of Sonnets to Bothwell with rather flowery translations by Bax with texts of the Casket letters. Despite some hilarious misprints, it was valuable as the only book containing a few of Mary's poems likely to turn up in second-hand bookshops at an affordable price.

PICTURE ACKNOWLEDGEMENTS: Courtesy of Astley House – Fine Art. Moreton-in-Marsh. Gloucestershire: page 42-3; *Photographie Bibliothèque Nationale, Paris*: page 20; *From His Grace the Duke of Atholl's Collection at Blair Castle, Perthshire*: pages 15, 70; *Glasgow Museums*: page 94; *Guildhall Art Gallery, Corporation of London/Bridgeman Art Library*: page 50-1; *Jersey Museums Service*: page 98; *Collection du Musée des Beaux-Arts du Château de Blois*: page 103; *National Galleries of Scotland*: pages 49, 65; *The Trustees of the National Library of Scotland*: pages 25, 109; *By courtesy of the National Portrait Gallery*: pages 22, 57, 58, ,63, 81; *National Trust Photographic Library*: pages 89, 91; *Perth Museum and Art Gallery*: page 70-1; *Rotherham Metropolitan Borough Council/Clifton Park Museum*: page 26; *Royal Collection, St James's Palace © Her Majesty The Queen*: pages 2, 10; *Scottish National Portrait Gallery*: pages 30, 74, 75, 82, 106; *By permission of the University of St Andrews*: page 86.

Mary, Queen of Scots. Vol XII. 31. Manuscript in Public Record Office. 1580 approx.

Texts of 'Cela Vraiment N'a Poinct De Courtoisie' and also 'Les Dieux, Les Cieux, La Mort'. First attributed to Mary by Marham Thorpe, who compiled the Record Office calendars for Mary's period.

Mary Stuart Archive Fc8 Nos 22-24. Manuscripts in Bodleian Library, Oxford. 1583, 1587 approx.

Texts of Sonnets in Prison I and II, Verses to Ronsard and Sonnet written at Fotheringhay Castle.

Vita Mariae Stuartae Scotiae Reginae. Georgius Conaeus (George Conn). Rome. 1624. p61.

Latin translation, possibly by George Buchanan, of 'The Diamond Speaks', a poem whose original French text is lost. I used both Chaloner's (see above) and Conn's Latin versions for my English translation to give me the clearest idea of what Mary wrote in French.

Vie Des Dames Illustres. Pierre de Bourdeilles, Seigneur de Brantôme. Leyden. 1665.

Text of the ode on the death of Francis II.

De Vita Et Rebus Gestiis Serenissimae Principis Mariae Scotorum Reginae. Samuel Jebb. London 1725. Vol II pp 23-24.

Text of the ode on the death of Francis II.

Receuil Des Lettres, Instructions Et Memoires De Marie Stuart. Vol VII p 346-352. Ed. Prince Alexandre Labanoff. 1844.

Texts of verses written in Mary's Book of Hours, the original of which was preserved in the Imperial Library in St Petersburg until the Russian Revolution in 1917 and is now in the M E Saltykov-Schedrin Library in St Petersburg MS Lat Q. V.I. 112. Photographs of the relevant leaves in the Book of Hours exist in the Advocates' Library of the National Library of Scotland. MS 81.55.

The Poems of Mary, Queen of Scots. Ed. Julian Sharman. London. 1873.

Texts of several of Mary's poems, but with many omissions. He gives no sources for his texts. He includes the Latin poem from Buxton Wells. He also quotes the two line poem supposedly written on a window in Fotheringhay Castle.

Poésies Françaises de Marie Stuart. M Pawlowsi. In *Le Livre,* Paris. 1873.

This article includes the quatrain written in her aunt's prayer book and the poem to the Bishop of Ross on his release from prison.

Queen Mary's Book. Ed. Mrs P Arbuthnott. London. 1907.

By far the most comprehensive and scholarly source book to date for Mary's poems. Although there are many omissions, she includes a large number of Mary's poems with translations by Agnes Strickland. In her zeal for Mary's cause, Mrs Strickland renders her words into a mixture of Gothic romanticism and Victorian hymn lyrics, often sacrificing sense for rhyme. To give Agnes Strickland her due, the occasional snippets of translation attempted by later writers such as Antonia Fraser have been no better.

The Poems Of Mary, Queen of Scots To The Earl of Bothwell. Ed. Joh Enschede en Zonen. Haarlem. 1932.

French texts of the Bothwell sonnets, including lines missing from the 'Detection' of 1571, i.e., line thirteen of 'Elle Pour Son Honneur' and line six of 'Mon Amour Croît'. It is a fine-edition Christmas gift booklet with only 250 copies, printed from the manuscript: VII.47.19 in the Cambridge University catalogue of manuscripts.

The Silver Casket. Ed. Clifford Bax. London. 1946.

Texts of Sonnets to Bothwell with rather flowery translations by Bax with texts of the Casket letters. Despite some hilarious misprints, it was valuable as the only book containing a few of Mary's poems likely to turn up in second-hand bookshops at an affordable price.

PICTURE ACKNOWLEDGEMENTS: Courtesy of Astley House – Fine Art. Moreton-in-Marsh. Gloucestershire: page 42-3; *Photographie Bibliothèque Nationale, Paris*: page 20; *From His Grace the Duke of Atholl's Collection at Blair Castle, Perthshire*: pages 15, 70; *Glasgow Museums*: page 94; *Guildhall Art Gallery, Corporation of London/Bridgeman Art Library*: page 50-1; *Jersey Museums Service*: page 98; *Collection du Musée des Beaux-Arts du Château de Blois*: page 103; *National Galleries of Scotland*: pages 49, 65; *The Trustees of the National Library of Scotland*: pages 25, 109; *By courtesy of the National Portrait Gallery*: pages 22, 57, 58, ,63, 81; *National Trust Photographic Library*: pages 89, 91; *Perth Museum and Art Gallery*: page 70-1; *Rotherham Metropolitan Borough Council/Clifton Park Museum*: page 26; *Royal Collection, St James's Palace © Her Majesty The Queen*: pages 2, 10; *Scottish National Portrait Gallery*: pages 30, 74, 75, 82, 106; *By permission of the University of St Andrews*: page 86.